T

2

TITANIA'S NUMBER

2

Titania Hardie

CONNECTIONS
BOOK PUBLISHING

For my sister, and my first-born

A CONNECTIONS EDITION
This edition published in Great Britain in 2007 by
Connections Book Publishing Limited
St Chad's House, 148 King's Cross Road, London WC1X 9DH
www.connections-publishing.com

British Library Cataloguing-in-Publication data available on request.

ISBN 978-1-85906-224-1

1 3 5 7 9 10 8 6 4 2

Phototypeset in Bliss and Natural Script using QuarkXPress on Apple Macintosh
Printed in China

Contents

STARTING THE JOURNEY

This little book of numerology invites you to be amazed by what you will learn from numbers – about your character, your tastes, your instincts, your relationships, and even about your future. But to do this involves a willingness to believe – as Pythagoras, the 'Father of Numbers' did – that numbers can provide a clue, or formula, through which we can perceive some of the evolving patterns and cycles that affect our own individual existence.
Let's find out more ...

Discovering numerology

Fans of Sudoku will understand how it entices us intellectually to see how strands of numbers – almost magically – slot together and interconnect with one another, revealing a rhythm of harmonious relationships between the lines. In one sense, numerology does this for us on a personal and spiritual level. The Science of Numbers, as it is called, suggests that there is an order and a rhythm in the universe of which we are a part, and although there is a certain mystery in the way numbers seem to function as symbols for our experiences, there is a long tradition across many cultures of their fascination for us.

Now, in an age of gigabytes, PINs and mathematic-based technology, how can we doubt the role that numbers play, or the way in which they have become part of our daily landscape? Numbers speak to us every day about

1 9 8 7 6 5 4 3 2

our personal identity on this planet. Our birth date is absorbed by society as proof of our existence: you need it to be 'real' at the bank, in the office, when you travel, in an automated phone queue – in *all* official records. Indeed, many people consider the day-date of their birthday to be their lucky number. But can it really say anything about us?

Did you know, for instance, that:

- If you were a **5** or a **9**, you'd need to invest in good-quality luggage because you'd be bound to notch up a lot of air miles?
- Or that a **6** feels compelled to generously host open-house for guests and family?
- A **7** will want to specialize in whatever interests them?
- And an **8** would rather have one small quality gift than half a dozen less luxurious presents?
- Or that any friend who's a **4** will painstakingly spend

2   3   4   5   6   7   8   9   1

hours getting something just right, whereas a **3** will have several projects on the go at one time and get through as best they can? C'est la vie!

But you've picked *this* little volume because you're a **2**, so, when it comes to business and personal relationships, a co-operative *partnership* is always desirable ... whereas, had you been a **1**, you would constantly be seeking significant personal freedom in your life and your career, and would prefer to work for yourself. **2** enjoys good team work!

About this book

Each individual title in this series investigates, in depth, the meaning of one of nine personal numbers. *This* volume is dedicated to the exploration of the number **2**.

We will be focusing principally on your **DAY** number – that is, the number relating to the day of the month on

1   9   8   7   6   5   4   3   2

which you were born (in your case, the 2nd, 11th, 20th or 29th of the month). Calculating your **DAY** number is easy: you simply add the digits of your day together (where applicable), and keep adding them until they reduce to a single number (*see calculation examples on page 270*). And that's it. It doesn't matter which month or year you were born in – you just need the day-date to discover your **DAY** number. And *you're* a **2**. (If you were born on the 11th or the 29th, this also gives you a 'master' number of **11**; we'll have something special to say about this later.)

Your **DAY** number reveals all kinds of information, and, working from this number, we will be considering:

- The obvious attributes of your number as they impact on your personality
- How you are likely to dress, and what colours or styles appeal
- What annoys you most

| 2 | 3 | 4 | 5 | 6 | 7 | 8 | 9 | 1 |

- How you react to things psychologically, and what drives or motivates you
- In which fields you will have the most natural abilities and gifts
- What sort of lover you are, and how you relate to all other numbers
- What the future holds

... and much, much more.

And you have another significant number too: your LIFE number. This is derived from adding up the digits in the *whole* of your birth date – day, month and year (*see examples on page 270*). What does *this* number mean, and what do your DAY and LIFE numbers mean in tandem? And how does it affect you if you're also a 'master' number (**11** or **22**)? Read on and you'll see. But first, let's meet your DAY number ...

1   9   8   7   6   5   4   3   2

So, you're a 2

Peacemaker, artist, co-worker, intuitionist, you are a **sensitive** soul who can be easily offended and deeply touched emotionally by the world and people around you; but you are also extremely **considerate** and kind towards those people. Though sometimes shy with strangers, you are often inspired by an '**inner light**' which makes you great company among your own friends, and much admired by them. Your greatest strength is that you can touch people with your words and tactfully **persuade** them to see your point of view – which is why you can make peace so brilliantly between discordant friends.

You can be self-conscious and also extraordinarily **stubborn**, but you have an obvious **sincerity** in your deal-

2   3   4   5   6   7   8   9   1

ings with the world and a **gentle**, spiritual side to your nature, which makes others trust you instinctively. Admired for your grace and aesthetic sense, you are usually **musical**, and may possibly dance well – especially as one of a pair. Ballroom dancing and romantic tangos may be just for you or, perhaps, playing musical duets and singing harmonies. You are the most generous and **accommodating** team-mate of all the numbers, and you will probably decide you are happiest working in tandem with others, both creatively and in career terms. You are inspired when bouncing your ideas off someone you can respect, and whom you can relate to well.

Certainly, you appreciate all the beautiful and **artistic** things in life – unless a lack of educational scope, or an unhelpful early life, has deprived you of exposure to them. When you are truly inspired, you have excellent taste – though you may be quite a **shameless romantic**. You feel deeply, and are highly alert to the nuances of your surroundings. However, this can mean that one of your difficult challenges will be to fight the tendency towards fluctuating **mood swings** and sudden depressions. You must try to overcome this, if possible. This moodiness may be because you so badly want – and need – affection from others, having so much to give, as well, and also because you sometimes **underestimate** your abilities and qualities. You mistakenly feel you must be 'needed' in a relationship, rather than simply allowing your right to just be loved. This **self-effacing** trait can usher you into emotional situations in which you make yourself a doormat for others. You will never feel a true sense of self-esteem this way!

Always aware of the foregoing presence of the masculine number **1**, **2** is a **feminine** number in the best sense. This does not suggest that women should take second place, but both the number and the feminine essence are instinctively **aware of others** in the world. **2** considers itself in relation to friends and loved ones. Traditionally a passive (though not inactive!) number, the number **2** came into its own with the new millennium, as it is now the leading digit in the date, bringing with it a powerful implication of **consideration** for others, and a respect for feminine intuition and **tact**.

With **2/11** as your principal, everyday number, you are probably able to work in positive **agreement** with those near you. You check daily details and gather up necessary facts. Whoever shares a house with you knows you can be over-sensitive and **easily hurt** – sometimes touchy! – but very **loyal**. **2**s consider their family's needs and opinions – although it can take time to arrive at simple decisions while you weigh up two arguments.

If you happen to have a name, or nickname, containing the letters B, K or T (each of which has a numerical value of **2** – more about which shortly), you will be able to harness the full power and best qualities of the number **2**, as it will help you to counter your **emotional tension** and nervousness. **2**'s closest astrological relative is the sign Cancer – somewhat stubborn, but gentle and **warm-hearted**.

Sound familiar? Getting a taste for what your number is about? And this is just the beginning. You'll soon find out how the number 2 expresses itself as your Day number in each and every day of your life. But before we go any further, let's take a look at where all this first came from . . .

What's in a number?

Numbers have always had a sacred meaning. The Egyptians used an alphabet that conflated letters and numbers, and, as such, each number exuded an idea that was more than the sum it stood for. There is a whole book of the Old Testament devoted to the subject; and the Hebrew language – exactly like the Egyptian – has a magical subtext of meaning where letters and numbers can be doubled to reveal an extra layer of secret, so-called 'occult' information. It is called the *gematria*, and forms a crucial part of the sacred occult wisdom called Kabbalah. There were twenty-two letters – a master number – in both the Greek (Phoenician) and Hebrew alphabets, and repetitions of the spiritual properties of the numbers **3** and, especially, **7** recur throughout the Bible.

1 9 8 7 6 5 4 3 2

The Father of Numbers

But modern numerology derives more formally from Pythagoras, the Father of Numbers, who was a serious and spiritual philosopher, as well as the man who explained some of the secrets of geometry. Born on the island of Samos, although he ultimately settled in Cretona, a Greek colony in southern Italy, he is understood to have travelled widely to both Egypt and Judea. Some accounts of his life also suggest he may have studied under the Persian sages of Zoroaster, but an analysis of his teachings certainly reveals the strong influence of Kabbalistic thought in his philosophy.

Pythagoras understood numbers as a *quality* of being, as well as a *quantity* of material value. In one sense, the numbers as figures were connected with the measuring of things, but 'number' itself was significantly different to this, and encompassed a spiritual value. The numbers from

2   3   4   5   6   7   8   9   1

one through to nine represented universal principles through which everything evolves, symbolizing even the stages an idea passes through before it becomes a reality. Mathematics was the tool through which we could apprehend the Creation, the universe, and ourselves. Musical harmony was a sacred part of this knowledge, as was geometry, which revealed divine proportion.

Most importantly, Pythagoras believed that numbers were expressive of the principles of all real existence – that numbers themselves embodied the principles of our dawning awareness, our conjecture and growth. Through mathematics and number we could approach divine wisdom and the workings of the universe as a macrocosm. Thus, in microcosm, our personal 'mathematics' would unlock the workings of our own being, and help us to see a divine wisdom concerning ourselves. **1** was not just the first digit, but also had a character of beginning, of independence, of leadership, just as the number **2** was more than merely the second number quantifying two objects, but also implied the philosophical concept of a pair, of co-operation, of a relationship beyond the individual.

Pythagoras also believed that we could understand our direction and fate through an awareness of repeating cycles of number, making numerology a key to revealing our opportunities and our destiny.

By tradition, the doctrine Pythagoras taught to his students in the sixth century BCE was secret, and no one wrote down his ideas until his death. But Plato was a follower of Pythagoras and, along with the rebirth of Platonism, the ideas of the Father of Mathematics were revealed afresh during the revival of Greek learning in the Renaissance. The great magi of the fifteenth and sixteenth centuries explored anew the significance of number and the gematria, to understand the hidden messages of the ancients and of the divine mind. Mathematics as a philosophy was the bridge to higher realms of spirituality.

2   3   4   5   6   7   8   9   1

Essence of the numbers

one is the spark, the beginning, Alpha, the Ego of consciousness. It is male.

two is consort. Adding partnership, receptivity, it is female, bringing tact.

three is a synthesizing of both of these qualities and brings expansion and joy.

four is the number of the Earth, of the garden, and of stability. It brings order.

five is curiosity and experiment, freedom, changes. It brings sensuality.

six nurtures and cares for others. It will love and beautify, and brings counsel.

seven perfects and contemplates the Creation. It is intellect, stillness, spirit.

eight is the number of power, the octave, a higher incarnation. It brings judgement.

nine is humanity, selflessness, often impersonal and all-knowing. It brings compassion.

1 9 8 7 6 5 4 3 2

Applying the knowledge

A deeper understanding of the self can be achieved through an awareness of the mysticism of number within us; and both the birth date and, to some degree, our given name are the keys to unlocking our mystical, spiritual core of being. Exploring the affinity between letter and number can also reveal insights about the lessons we need to learn throughout our lives to improve and develop as individuals (*see page 25*).

This book looks at the significance of numbers as they affect us every day, focusing largely, as introduced earlier, on our **DAY** number. It is this number that reveals to us our instincts, our impulses, our natural tastes and undiluted responses, our talents and immediate inclinations. This is how people see us in daily situations, and how we behave by essence.

We will be exploring how our **DAY** number influences

2   3   4   5   6   7   8   9   1

our love relationships and friendships; at what it says about our career strengths and our childhood; at the way our number manifests in our leisure time; and at how it might give us a better understanding of what to expect in our future cycles, as we pass through any given year under the sway of a particular number. Each birthday initiates a new cycle, and each cycle seems uncannily connected with the philosophical concerns of the number which governs that year. Look both to the past and present to see how strongly the number-cycle can illuminate our experiences ... and then count ahead to ponder what may be in store over the next year or two.

And numbers also say something about where we live or work, about our car, and even about our pets. Understanding these secret qualities can add a new dimension of pleasure — not to mention surprise — to our journey through life.

1 9 8 7 6 5 4 3 2

A NUMBER TO GROW INTO

The presence of our **LIFE** number, however, takes longer for us to appreciate in ourselves – longer for us to grow into – and it often takes time to reveal itself. This number comes to the fore as your life progresses, and on pages 214–247 we will be looking at the meaning of your **DAY** number together with your individual **LIFE** number, to see what this reveals about your character and potentiality.

The **LIFE** number may intensify the experience of the **DAY** number – if it is closely related to it, or shares similar patterns. But more frequently our two different numbers clash a little, and this often allows insight into the aspects of our being where instinct pulls us in one direction but higher wisdom or experience mediates and pulls us in a second direction.

Who would have thought you could learn so much from a number? Pythagoras certainly did, over 2,500 years ago … and now you will discover it too.

2   3   4   5   6   7   8   9   1

What's in a name?

Your name also has a story to tell, and it is a story revealed through number. Every letter corresponds to a number: in the Western alphabet we use twenty-six letters, which are at variance with the twenty-two formerly enshrined in the Hebrew and Greek alphabets. Some numerologists believe that this is in keeping with the more material world we now live in, as the number '26' reduces to '8' (when you add the digits), which is the number of power and money.

The correspondences between the numbers and the letters of the alphabet are as follows:

1	2	3	4	5	6	7	8	9
A	B	C	D	E	F	G	H	I
J	K	L	M	N	O	P	Q	R
S	T	U	V	W	X	Y	Z	

1	9	8	7	6	5	4	3	2

As you are a **2**, it is most revealing to look at the letters B, K and T, as they occur (or not!) in your name. This is because they intensify the experience and impression of your main number.

To make the most of the qualities inherent in your number, you should be using a name which is in poetic harmony with your **DAY** number. As a **2**, you will most effectively tap into the diplomacy and persuasiveness you need to act on your excellent instincts and analytical skills if you have a name that underlines these **2** qualities. Using a name which includes a B, K or T sharpens your senses. If this sounds strange, consider that many of us have our names shortened or played upon by friends, family and lovers, so it is important to feel that our chosen name – the one that we use as we go about in the world – is making the best of our abilities and energies.

Among the letters that are equivalent to the number **2**, T is a common consonant, so the chances are that you

2   3   4   5   6   7   8   9   1

have this letter in your name. It is very significant if your name starts with one of these letters, for it introduces the strength of your number right at the beginning of your name. And if you were born on the 11th or 29th, making you an **11** (master number) variation of the **DAY** number **2**, the letter K is the only one which corresponds completely to your number. Create a nickname with it in, if necessary, just to back up the outstanding properties of the **11** that we'll talk about later in this book!

The letter-numbers help us to act out our sense of purpose, and if these work in correspondence with the **DAY** number we are more likely to find our sense of will and achieve our goals more rapidly. But if we have few, or none, of the letters of our **DAY** number, we often feel it is much harder to shine in our field of opportunity. Let's take a closer look at what this means ...

Missing a '2' letter?

As a **2**, you will find you reach your career potential more easily if your work name includes one of the above letters. But, as a **2**, living up to your talents for co-work can be draining. Your number rarely seeks leadership, and understands the necessity of listening to others. But if your name lacks a '**2**' letter, you may find that others take advantage of you, and fail to give you your due for the work you contribute.

This will be just as true in relationships, where your desire to prioritize another's needs becomes an expectation for which you are never appreciated. You will rail and grumble, and become too inward-looking, if the name you use is without a '**2**' letter somewhere. A simple variation in the spelling of your name could change this, and mean that you learn how to assert your gentle manoeuvring skills, and feel you are being listened to and acknowledged.

| 2 | 3 | 4 | 5 | 6 | 7 | 8 | 9 | 1 |

Your peers and family can even give you a pet name, if necessary, to offset any imbalance.

Too many T's?

It can be just as much of a problem if your name carries a flood of letters which correspond to your number. This potentially gives you an overdose, and brings out some of the negative qualities associated with **2**.

A lot of 'T's in the name you use can make you too manipulative, or can work against your strengths, so that you fail to communicate with your love partner clearly. **2**s look at what is going on behind the obvious, but not everyone is on your wavelength, and you may feel as though you're talking to the wall sometimes! Equally, a name with many 'B's can go to great heights and great depths emotionally. Lose one of these '**2**' letters if you have too many in your name!

| 1 | 9 | 8 | 7 | 6 | 5 | 4 | 3 | 2 |

YOUR DAY NUMBER
It's a new day ...

You will learn a lot about the numbers of your birthday and your name as this book unfolds, but the DAY number is, to my mind, the most important – and sometimes least well-recognized – number of all ... the number which exerts a magnetic hold on us each and every day of our lives. Every time we react to a situation, an emotion, a provocation of any kind, we are shooting straight from the hip, as it were, and this reaction is coloured by our DAY number.

As we know, your 'Day Force', or DAY, number is **2** if you were born on the 2nd, 11th, 20th or 29th of any month. Each of these different dates also affects us – the charac-

| 2 | 3 | 4 | 5 | 6 | 7 | 8 | 9 | 1 |

teristics of the number derived from a birthday on the 11th vary intriguingly from one on the 20th, for instance (especially given the added master-number dimension) — and we will look at these differences in the pages ahead.

All four dates, however, still reconcile to an overall 2. This number determines your gut reactions and the way you express yourself when you are being most true to yourself. Your parents, lovers, friends and co-workers all know you best through this number.

So what is the theme of being a 2? What are you like when you're at work, rest and play? And how compatible are you with the other numbers? Let's find out ...

1 9 8 7 6 5 4 3 2

2'S CHARACTER
Charms, graces, warts and all ...

Inherent in the concept of the number **2** is the idea that there is more than one person in this world – more than one idea to grasp. Very distinctly from the number **1**, yours is a number which places other people in the everyday vision. Not only are you sensitive to the needs and wishes of others, but you run the risk of being almost too accommodating and conscious of their position – sometimes to the detriment of your own life! You see below the surface of their speech and expression, knowing when there are contradictions in what they profess to believe or feel. This makes you a born diplomat and tactician, intuiting any other person's true situation almost before they are even aware of it themselves.

| 2 | 3 | 4 | 5 | 6 | 7 | 8 | 9 | 1 |

Although you can project a mild and peaceful nature, you can be surprisingly forceful when you have your mind bent on something. Anyone thinking you're a pushover who can easily be manipulated will find you a tower of unexpected strength; and, when it comes to creating the kind of dynamic between people where things can be done and progress achieved, you are the natural choice.

Gently does it

2 is frequently seen as the gentle soul of the world, but there is a power in that gentleness which can move mountains. Many politicians or people working in the foreign office are born on **2** days, and your negotiation skills are second to none. You are always aware of opposites – personalities, arguments, debates, philosophies. Since childhood, you have progressed through the world listening attentively, and learning without talking your head off, so

1   9   8   7   6   5   4   3   2

you have a deeply tuned sense of what is really happening when any number of people come together. This can make it hard for you to choose a position, but you are always fair to both sides.

Your number is highly spiritual, which does not necessarily mean you are drawn to traditional religious ideas, but rather that you are alert to the stirrings of life and light everywhere around you. Because you are so determined to create peace in your environment, you have a way of persuading more aggressive people to your position. Your number brings disparate interests together for common accord, and your talent to achieve this feeling of unity makes you, perhaps, the number with the greatest capacity for insight.

You will gain many allies, and make lasting friendships, because of your understanding of the complexities of people and things, and you will find that, most often, your wishes come true without pushing too hard. Everything

2   3   4   5   6   7   8   9   1

best that comes to you comes *gently*. Patience is a virtue you will gain more and more as you get older, and you will soon come to realize that you can attract many good things — and people — into your life like a magnet, rather than pursuing what you want head-on. You are talented and perceptive, and you recognize the needs of many people, rather than only one or two.

Keynotes of the 2 personality

Positive associations: modesty, inner strength, calming effect on others, aesthetic taste, diplomatic skills, heightened awareness of others' feelings, meditative powers, understanding partner, musical

Negative associations: overly timid, self-annihilating, negative, over-worrying, high expectations of partners, not knowing how to stand up for your own rights, time-wasting, martyrdom, not expressing irritations with others

1 9 8 7 6 5 4 3 2

Happy harmony

Not only do you love what is beautiful, but you also create beauty everywhere around you. Even when down to your last penny you will somehow find a budget to buy fresh flowers for the house, or perfume for your spirit. You are not generally acquisitive, but beautiful things around you inspire your gentleness and your artistic imagination, so aesthetic objects are often vital to your sense of well-being.

If you have a number **4** anywhere in your birthday numbers, or if your partner is a **4**, or if you have several '**4**' letters (D, M or V) in your name, you will find this aesthetic taste is strongly expressed in your home and garden, which you want to make into a haven of tranquillity for everyone.

As harmony between people – or between yourself and others – is paramount in your idea of a happy life, you also have an appreciation for harmony in music, and **2**s often have an exceptional talent and taste for music or dance. It is sad if you feel this, and yet these talents have remained untrained, although music may be something you can still take time to develop over the years. In any case, your own music library is likely to be considerable and varied. **2**s also often like to spend time in art galleries, or actively engaged with other creative media, having a natural talent for drama and film, as they are able to feel another person's role so acutely. Your good taste will always influence the vocation you are in, and the appreciation friends have for you.

One of your best talents is the ability to gather details and facts from a variety of sources, and to make accurate assessments of what is good or bad about any set of circumstances. If you are asked to investigate whether there is any potential in a project, or any likelihood of building on a starting point, you are very astute in knowing the answer. You look behind the obvious and see what is missing, and you are never dissuaded from work just because the glory may not come to you from a project completed.

You are a superb team-player, and even when congratulated by peers and superiors your natural modesty means that you will try to play down all the fuss. You are concerned with the craft, or the job, and not the accolade; and your sincerity and lack of concern for public posturing is winning!

A sensitive soul

Love relationships can be a rollercoaster ride for you because you are so sensitive to what others are feeling, and yet you may be hurt that those same people are unaware of what *you* are thinking or going through. Selfishness in others is something you have no time for, and you can become disillusioned by the shallowness of certain people. You will have to become a little more assertive with both friends and lovers if you are not to feel taken advantage of, and occasionally steel yourself to ask for what you want.

2 is a paradox in this respect – that you have such wisdom and clarity about how those around you are feeling, and yet you lack self-confidence in some surprising ways. When others let you down (as they inevitably will, at times), your feelings get hurt, and you may even react as though you've been betrayed. This is where you may have to recognize that there are drawbacks in being too dependent on someone else. If you are pushed to it, your temper can explode, and amaze everyone!

For people who are dominant and aggressive, you may seem very easy-going and malleable. While it is true that you are happy following someone you respect and admire, it is also the case that you are careful where you place your loyalty and beliefs. You are very astute at identifying those who are entirely self-interested, and these people can never count on your support. You are not an egotist, but you are discerning, and you know what is right morally. You also see beauty and strength in people who are not always admired by the populace at large, because you see what is not obvious to everyone else. Male **2**s are lucky with women, as all **2**s find much to admire that is regarded as 'feminine', including feminine strength and versatility. You have an amazing power to detach yourself from certain emotional positions and circumstances, and see both objectively and deeply. You are gentle, perhaps, but nobody's fool.

Balancing act

You are generally a very adaptable person, able to jump in a different direction without feeling any pain. This makes you ideally suited to jobs which require a middle-man who

2   3   4   5   6   7   8   9   1

can settle disputes — negotiators, agents, lawyers, or even television presenters who have to balance different viewpoints among their guests! Unfortunately, this ability to find a middle ground means that friends select you as the go-between in many uncomfortable situations, and you may, at times, feel caught between the devil and the proverbial sea.

However, if anyone can engineer a meeting of minds it is you, and this talent may be the characterizing role that determines your fate on hundreds of occasions. Vocationally, it gives you the right temperament for personnel management and talent-scouting, and you will often find yourself luckiest — and happiest — in industries that relate to providing services and products for women, or anything otherwise deemed feminine.

Perhaps you are drawn to design — if not as a career, then as a hobby or sideline. You may also flourish in government jobs, or teaching, or any work which puts others first. Though you're not aggressive about rising through the ranks in what you do, your charm is likely to see you gain eminence without trying too hard anyway.

And the downside?

Yes – there are negatives with your number. If anyone makes the mistake of underestimating your tenacity, they're likely to rue the day. You can dish out some quite blunt speech and pithy maxims if you feel criticized or ignored, and you can even be an extremist about what you like or what you want, or will or won't do. Moreover, when you're really involved in ideas for a project you've been set or a plan you have embarked on, you can be dogmatic, argumentative and impossible to reason with.

You don't forget hurts, although you will agree to create peace: but your goodwill, once lost, is lost forever. Add to this the fact that you are (perhaps through intu-

2   3   4   5   6   7   8   9   1

ition) inclined to form strong likes and dislikes, apparently without reason, and you will confuse and confound many people who love you!

Sometimes you manage to work yourself into a corner through your irrational feelings — and then you need rescuing from yourself. You may also be indecisive at key moments, or vacillate between two completely opposite courses of action or direction. Very occasionally, a **2** may even be deceitful or two-faced, but this is only going to happen in the event of an extremely unhappy and confused soul. For the most part, **2**s are well-loved and loving, giving a great deal of themselves, and being given to by those who love them.

Be prepared!

2s have a distinctive personal style, and are usually highly popular and attractive to the opposite sex. If you know yourself well, you might admit you can be very finicky about fashion details and accessories, and everything has to be just so! You prefer to be neat and clean, and you are happiest functioning in order and tranquillity.

You will take trouble to decorate your office or home, desk or even car, with tiny classy details that tell the world discreetly of your grace and charm. And you also take your time over dressing, creating your image for the day – not because of ego so much as a need to bolster your own confidence. You are happy when you feel properly prepared. **2** women seem to have both a nail file and needle and cotton in their handbag, while **2** men somehow always have an emergency toothbrush or razor for any occasion!

The image you project to most people is of calm modesty, and even if you choose to dress modestly you will be neat and harmonized in your appearance. **2**s automatically balance their fashion sense – a colour at the throat

2   3   4   5   6   7   8   9   1

will be echoed at the feet, or with another accessory. And **2** men are just as particular; co-ordination is as natural to you as breathing. Your taste is probably for relaxed styles that are easy to wear and look elegant rather than overly fussy or sculpted, but you always draw quiet admiration for your 'look'.

A lot to give

Perhaps the most distinctive quality of anyone with a **2** **DAY** number is the genuine ability to care for others, and to put other people's needs in perspective with their own life. They often give too much, and so make excellent parents and nurses, teachers and instructors, and they have a lovely sense of humour, which often takes people by surprise. Neither boisterous nor noisy, and not demanding nor attention-seeking, **2**s still thrive most when they are appreciated and quietly applauded.

1 9 8 7 6 5 4 3 2

Anyone living close to you will know that you are a rare soul with a tremendous spirit and seemingly inexhaustible sympathy. It is this which so often picks up other 'strong' numbers when they are down. By turns, you are offended and irritable, kindly and companionable, always intelligent and graceful. The number **2** is, to me, the 'thornless' rose of the number sequence.

2 in a nutshell

Personality watchwords: introvert, tactician, conciliatory nature

Lucky colours: pink gold, salmon, white (especially for 11/2s)

Lucky herbs/flowers: white rose, myrtle, white poppy, melissa (lemon balm)

Scents: rose, green tea, carnation, cinnabar

Fashion style: elegant colours, tactile fabrics, well co-ordinated

Decorative style: feminine, harmonizing, pastels/soft whites, romantic

Letters: B, K or T (needed in the name you use)

Car style: elegant classic; quietly expensive but not vulgar

Holiday destination: near the sea

1 9 8 7 6 5 4 3 2

Which 2 are you?

7 8 9 1 **2** 3 4 5 6

Everyone with a day number of **2** will exhibit many of the characteristics just discussed. It is interesting to see, though, how the number **2** varies across all of its incarnations. There is a subtle but definite difference between the way the number operates for someone born on the 2nd of the month – which makes for a pure **2** effect – and someone born, say, on the 29th.

As a rule, anyone born on the single-digit date has the truest and most undiluted effect from the number, whereas someone born as a product of two digits borrows some qualities from the pairing of the numbers. Specifically, there is a real dynamism which comes with

2 3 4 5 6 7 8 9 1

the numbers **11** and **29**, but twenty-anything puts the softening digit '2' before the second number, and this usually means that, whatever number you are, you are more aware of the needs of others. Similarly, if '1' is the first digit (11th), you are more independent, and perhaps more assured of your self-worth, than **2** people are generally.

Let's look at the variations across all the birthdays . . .

1 9 8 7 6 5 4 3 2

Born on the 2nd?

A gentle and inspired soul who has a real inner light from your earliest years, you are the purest **2**. You have a natural wish to live peacefully in love, both with your family and in your workplace, and if this is denied you, you may become frustrated and grumpy – though it's not part of your true nature to be so! You can achieve exactly what you want through skilful diplomacy, without ever having to resort to force or aggression. Your exceptional perspicacity with others, and of the human condition, ensures you understand how to gently sway friends and loved ones without overheating. You're not really the outstanding or obvious executive type, but are the brilliant ambassador, often accomplishing what no one else can in terms of mediation. If there is any common ground between two disparate parties, you will discover and utilize it.

| 2 | 3 | 4 | 5 | 6 | 7 | 8 | 9 | 1 |

Appreciative of your non-aggressive honesty, everyone depends upon you to tell the truth, which you (mostly) do very tactfully. You support your friends in a crisis without expecting special gratitude, and bring a subtle supportive strength to your love partnerships, and reassurance to your children. You know just how to soothe and encourage, but you are also usually quite impartial, which makes you a good counsellor and friend to both sides. You like to be led, but are not in the least weak. Rather, you have a clear understanding of how to gain what you want without being coarse or blunt. Anger is a waste for you, and you would rather get by without unnecessary use of it. However, aggressive souls who think you are a pushover and unlikely to stand up for yourself are in for a shock! You talk them around without them noticing that you've quietly taken the upper hand and removed them from their tall horse.

You are gifted musically, having an excellent ear and often a gentle or melodic speaking voice. As an actor, you take direction well and need not be offered the leading role! You also love objects and places of beauty, and you manage to create a visual oasis of calm around you wherever you are – whether at work or at home, or even, perhaps, on a bus or plane. Something you carry within has the capacity to transform any space into a zone of tranquillity and beauty.

You work at your best in a partnership, aware of the process by which an idea can be generated by one person and developed by another. You have the sense to consult those closest to you, and know how to incorporate their ideas and wishes alongside your own harmonious overview. With such an accommodating personality you find it easy to devise ways of sharing your space and adjusting your taste to everyone's mutual satisfaction. And all this you do without fanfare or excessive fuss!

Many positions are open to you career-wise. We'll be looking at this in more detail in the next section, but, in brief, your excellent diplomatic skills and conciliatory nature make you a valued politician or civil servant. Equally, antiques, objects of beauty and subjects centred on fashion or art may appeal to you in business; and, since you are the perfect co-worker, you would be successful in any business partnership, provided you choose the right field. You can find pleasure in the simplest tasks, if they bring order and beauty when executed.

From the artistic point, poetry, writing, music, painting and sculpture will be your strongest suits. Creating gardens as a place for personal meditation or peace would also excite you. Facing the more mundane tasks when required is not a problem, and you bring a degree of perfection and excellence to banal duties: hence, book-keeping, statistics, secretarial work or research requiring analytical ability are all fields open to you. Whatever you choose, you will draw an appreciative smile from those who work around you.

1   9   8   7   6   5   4   3   2

Born on the 11th?

This is our first so-called master number, and it is granted a separate understanding from the ordinary digit **2**. It is not usually reduced to the simpler number because the powerful properties of the pair of linked **1**s – though they have an underlying personality of **2** – are at odds with the gentler, more passive **2**. These digits harness the strengths of two **1**s and have similar energies and aggressions, while they nevertheless contain the implicit spirit of **2**. Confused? This is partly why they are treated distinctly.

Both **11**s – your date, and that of the 29th – are tasked with looking at a greater picture, considering the future plans of the world. You will always be reaching beyond the personal, beyond the mundane, beyond the everyday. This can be a testing number for its holders, who must learn how to handle the 'double voltage' of living with both digits all the time. It does not often bring personal stability, and demands considerable mental acuity — to which end a good education is crucial. You also need strength of character, and sometimes have to place yourself philosophically at a distance from life and other people. Their rules will not be yours, and their lot not yours, either. However, the number **11** brings deep talents, extraordinary insights and huge personal stamina. It is *the* number of intuition, wisdom and exceptional performance.

With a birthday on the 11th, yours is the pure masternumber birthday. This is both good news and bad, as carrying this number anywhere in your personal numbers (perhaps even in your LIFE number, which we'll come to much later; *see page 214*) imports weighty responsibilities and tests, along with added possibilities. You have determination, but your wishes and wants fluctuate. Unlike a pure **2**, you love the limelight, and come alive in this situation; and you must allow yourself plenty of scope to vent

1 9 8 7 6 5 4 3 2

your inspirational ideas. Focus your energy and concentration so that you're an *achiever* and not just a *dreamer*.

You're a nervous perfectionist, highly strung, though to the world you appear calm and centred, like a true **2**. Psychic, you visualize things clearly, and have strong instincts. You must bring your intellect and intuition into balance. You will have a high standard of morals, which may even be conservative, but you should fight against imposing these attitudes on others too stringently.

Emotionally, you may be an extremist, caring deeply and protectively for your loved ones. Your criticism of others is most likely acute, but you will take umbrage if anyone criticizes those closest to you. You *are* out of the ordinary, with an excellent imagination. What is attainable, what is normal, what is a personal standard for you is on a higher plane than most people would be content with. Be careful of self-deceit, however, and work to discern fantasy from fact. Of course, what *is* truth and what *is* illusion

| 2 | 3 | 4 | 5 | 6 | 7 | 8 | 9 | 1 |

may form the nucleus of a very interesting debate for you.

You can succeed in, literally, any field which brings you before the public, ideal mediums being publishing, radio or television, music, dance or theatre, philosophy, art and art history, film, lecturing, advertising and PR work. Whatever gives you the opportunity to have your own business — preferably in something not too 'nine to five' — will suit your energy swings and ability to work tirelessly in long periods of time at a stretch. Humdrum work deadens your spirit and makes you lazy, possibly even making you cynical with the world and, consequently, a poor friend to anyone. Strive for something 'special' all the time, so that you can make an important contribution with your talents.

An **11** birthday synthesizes the power and courage inherent in **1** with the persuasive skill and sensitivity of **2**. These paired gifts could enable you to truly make a mark in the world ... but they also confer twice as much responsibility and potential for dissatisfaction.

1   9   8   7   6   5   4   3   2

Born on the 20th?

A person who seems to have accepted that life entails service to others and the necessity to be a good listener rather than voicing your own views or woes, you are an especially tactful 2, diplomatic and strongly devoted to your family and loved ones. The most gifted peacemaker of the 2s, if you live with your positive energies you have the power to succeed at anything you're inclined to try; but, if your upbringing and conditioning have made you more negative, this may well mean that you're changeable and unreliable.

With ten times the drive and potential of the single-digit 2, you have a particularly finely honed appreciation of music and of the arts generally, and a beautiful, subtle feeling for colour. You will be driven to read, to watch, to listen, to be aware of what the world offers in a cultured landscape. Many people born on the 20th choose to work in publishing, television, film or theatre, or in the music industry. You may not feel driven to contribute the creative work itself so much as possessing an appreciation and comprehension of the work of others; and you are drawn to really talented and creative people who need your powers of diplomacy and introductory skills in order to flourish themselves.

You are loving and sympathetic and enjoy nature, the countryside and your home. Just as you are good at bringing peace, you need to find places of peace to recharge your own batteries, and help you unwind from the stresses of modern living. Your own personality, environment and way of doing things embodies grace, style and beauty; and you incorporate music, art and loveliness in the world you create around you. Though not at all garish, your style is distinctive – and often witty. The crucial rule, though, is balance. An inharmonious dwelling place,

1   9   8   7   6   5   4   3   2

or office climate, will make you very stressed and unhappy, and not allow you to perform at your peak.

Career-wise, you would succeed in any field of public work – particularly as an analyst, teacher (possibly of humanities, or art- or music-related subjects), or actor; and, quite differently, as a clergyman, politician, statistician, a musician proper, a clerk, or even a stenographer. You would ideally make the best of politicians; however, you may write more effectively than you speak, so may prefer to be behind the scenes rather than the front runner. You can be extremely patient in handling detail, thus could ably handle estates, or succeed in corporate law/politics.

You would, in fact, be very well suited to top-secret government work, with your innate sense of diplomacy and reliability, but are often quite content to work in small groups or for others, tending not to push for your own business or personal supremacy. This sometimes means others depend too strongly on you, expecting you to do the difficult leg work while they push themselves forward to take all the credit. However, you view this philosophically, and don't always consider it worth fighting over.

The basic **2** element is with you tenfold: femininity (even in men, who are gentle beings with many women as friends!), intuition and a giving nature (indeed, your strongly loving nature can allow others to take advantage of you); and you will often place others before yourself. This birthday corresponds to the receptive female, moon principle. You co-operate with others by nature, and are born to be in a loving pair – making you a real 'catch' as a marriage partner.

1   9   8   7   6   5   4   3   2

Born on the 29th?

The 29th is the other **11** master-number birthday. You can achieve much in this lifetime, but you will also face daily tests along the way. Your true destiny places you before the public; idealist and dreamer, you have great capacities for leadership. You may be strongly spiritual, possessing instinctive wisdom and an innate philosophy. And for you there's no such thing as impossibility! The world is a realm of dreams from which you can draw any one and make it your own; you can establish contact with any person (even in the highest office) and ask for information, attain any post or place of dwelling without the slightest notion that it may be beyond usual reach. You work from the deepest levels of intuition, knowing at a glance who to trust and what project is sound and what is silly; and you have, perhaps, the most original mind of all the numbers, drawing on the creative vision of number **9** with the power of **2** to get on with the job quietly.

You must be the leader in your group or business: there is no point doing anything to get ordinary results. As a child you would have been bored by plodders and wished for adult status immediately. You recognize no class or capability differences between yourself and anyone else – which can sometimes border on rebelliousness! You are destined for mastery – but only if you use your gifts fully. A **29/11** is like a high-IQ child – immensely bright but often lazy. Be challenged, and push yourself hard. Then, the sky is the limit.

Both sceptical of what sounds irrational and perceptive of what may appeal in a visionary way, you motivate others easily and are a superb educator or public speaker, whipping up enthusiasm among otherwise stale people. You should become famous, widely known within bounds – but this fame is for public good rather than self-glory.

1   9   8   7   6   5   4   3   2

Achieve this balance and your life will be rich beyond measure (in every sense).

You have a tendency to worry and over-analyse, and can be self-willed. You must also avoid a propensity to be so enthralled in your own world that you ignore others' strife. Try to keep calm and balanced. You have many friends and love all the beautiful things in life, and need a stable and sympathetic house to come home to. You can convince anyone of anything, if you've a mind to; however, you must fight your intolerance of those who cannot grasp things as quickly or easily as you. It is perfectly possible for you to have a hugely successful life, provided you remember other people's feelings!

This is a prosperous birthday number if you are wisely organized personally. The correct course for any master number is to help others, so you need to walk a straight path and help friends to do the same. You may be moody, depressive and nervous, but cultivating relaxation interests

2   3   4   5   6   7   8   9   1

will keep your spirits buoyant. This is especially true in love matters, for, like all of the 'double-digit' numbers, your emotions and feelings will run in extremes, and you will influence others with your mood. Learn to live in the real world, with a mortal human being for a partner rather than an idealized god. Be wise about yourself and your needs.

You should be drawn to a public career, such as acting, politics, public relations, music, lecturing, selling and marketing; but you will also add your own brand of professionalism to demanding secretarial work, writing, art, or office management. Again, as with the 11th (*see page 54*), utilize the dual powers of your originality and individuality that come from the **1**s in your number, together with the ability for tact and consideration of others that comes from the **2**, your base number.

1 9 8 7 6 5 4 3 2

2 AT WORK

So, what kind of employee does your number make you? We've already seen that your birthday suggests you are much more comfortable working in a close partnership, but when you are in a large group, how do you fit in? If you're the boss, are you a good one? Which fields are likely to be the best for your talents? And which the worst? And what about the male/female divide? Is a 2 female boss more desirable than a 2 male colleague?

Here, we get to grips with your career potential, your needs and 'must-have's for job satisfaction, and your loves and loathes work-wise, hopefully highlighting some areas where there is room for you to adjust your manner around others, to help you achieve what it is you're aiming for.

In the marketplace

Your number might be deemed the 'I feel' of numerology, rather like the first Water sign of the zodiac, Cancer. This means that, whether as corporation owner or floor-worker on the way up, you are aware always of the other people working around you, and of the market you are trying to satisfy. You will avoid angry exchanges whenever possible, both with your colleagues and with those you must please, but you are perfectly able to stand your ground if you believe something strongly enough!

If you work in a partnership, you will be the reliable soul whom everyone looks up to – the senior manager who is always prepared to make the tea or empty the bins, if necessary. You are rarely high-handed or reluctant to be 'one of the team' – even if it is your own business you've built up from scratch.

1   9   8   7   6   5   4   3   2

JOB SATISFACTION

Vocational direction is very important to you, because job satisfaction is crucial to your everyday feelings about life. We have already touched on your high moral standards, and you are unlikely to prosper in any work environment where you're at odds with the aims of the business or the people steering its course. You like financial security, but couldn't turn a blind eye to the source of the income. Therefore, you need to spend some time settling on your future path, because you will only be happy if you are doing something you believe in. Similarly, no matter how attractive an offer of work or an opening for your study, you'll turn it down if there is any conflict with the overall aims of the group around you. You – more than anyone – need to respect your peers and feel that the company has integrity.

Where a **1** will be the worker on the rise from day one, you're a dark horse about promotional chances. The strange thing is, you seem very gentle and not at all pushy about rising high; yet, you have such a skill at guessing others' needs, or realizing potential pitfalls before they occur, that you may find yourself thrust into a senior position or given independence without asking for it. If a **2** at work is rarely the declared team captain or figurehead, they are very frequently the crucial linchpin of any company. You are diligent, have excellent instincts and are unexceptionable to those you deal with, so everyone loves you!

WHERE DOES YOUR LIGHT REALLY SHINE?

Here are some of the qualities that **2**s bring to any job:

- A sharp logical mind and an excellent sense of your own organization and space give you the edge over companions in disarray, and you really love the challenge of working in a small select group where you can share your ideas. Partnerships suit you well.
- You have such superb intuition that others will consult you regularly for your reactions to products, people

and a balance of talent. You could be that highly paid personal assistant without whom the politician or Hollywood star could not function!

- You appreciate the beautiful things in life, and you should let this direct your fate in work terms. Not only do you need a good salary, but you will really achieve excellence if you select an industry that supplies aesthetic objects or services to the world. You see value where others do not, and you will be lucky in a career that serves women.

- You have the power to put two and two together, so you are sometimes at your best working in an environment which allows you to 'spy out' or intuit the unknown! Your relative lack of ego means you will take up positions that bring little thanks for the work, too.

- You comply at work with anyone who is polite, but manners are important to you, so it is fair that you insist upon them. Let your taste guide your choices.

| 2 | 3 | 4 | 5 | 6 | 7 | 8 | 9 | 1 |

All of these make you a person with unlimited skills and options. Where certain numbers have just one or two really clear lines of endeavour in which they will fly high, you can make a success of almost any course of work that allows you the kind of scope outlined above.

In any vocational path which demands you develop new contacts, clients or projects, you are in your element. Careers that work well with this kind of talent include ...

The arts: fashion industry, music, talent management
Even if your own artistic gifts have been sadly neglected or untrained in your childhood, you have the sensitivity to handle others with discretion and charm, so you would be perfect in all the people-related aspects of the arts. Managing, casting and directing musicians, dancers and actors would be another vent for your own creative talents, as ego never gets in your way. You would also be excellent front-of-house for a fashion house.

1 9 8 7 6 5 4 3 2

Medicine, healing, counselling Many **2**s make wonderful doctors or specialists in health care, as they are naturals at taking care of others without expecting enormous accolades in return. Any detailed work – laboratory skills or fine surgery, or a specialist secretary to a consultant – will suit you, and you are superb at working in tandem with others in a team for the complete welfare of a patient.

Banking and finance Your appreciation for the necessity of doing careful work makes you an excellent contributor to any field which demands the understanding of highly complex fiduciary knowledge. Banking and accounting, contracting and legalities concerning money, financial advice or the business of pensions – all suit **2**'s careful mind and concern for others.

PR and hosting skills Being the most charming of numbers, you and number **6** people could be the secret resource which gives any business the edge when a diplomatic public relations job is needed. Your goodwill and personality win over all comers.

Teaching and research work This suits you superbly, especially if you are a parent and want time to spend with your own family. **2**s teach naturally, and are usually quite patient, so this is an ideal line of work for you. You give a great deal and are delighted to be thanked in any way at all.

Beauty industry Services which pamper both men and women and provide an aesthetic haven from the pressured world are going to appeal to you, and **2**'s sensitive awareness of exactly what others need means that you will achieve innovations in the beauty or spa-therapy industry. Developing products for these industries and creating a magical sanctuary will come easily, and you may be drawn to working for yourself – in partnership – in such an area.

1   9   8   7   6   5   4   3   2

Hospitality and travel 2 knows how to please and cosset its clients, and nothing is too much trouble, so you are well suited to some kind of work in this field. If you're looking for a business partner, choose a **6**, whose skills dovetail with yours perfectly!

Art galleries and museums These are a source of great pleasure and interest for your number, so this is a domain which might entice you. **2**s are often found keeping records and minding – as well as curating – collections and antiquities.

IT Not glamorous, but the steady drive to get the work done efficiently and with attention to detail suits your mind and pattern of work hours. If you are a parent, you may decide to work from home, working flexible hours to suit your family.

2 3 4 5 6 7 8 9 1

This list isn't exhaustive – a **2** may make partnerships and find expression of interest in a diverse number of fields – but it does offer a good idea of the kinds of subject that should appeal to your number.

And for luck?

Whatever your work, you will achieve your maximum potential if you use a name to work with that includes the letters B, K or T. Remember this when you are choosing a company name, if you go into partnership. It will help, too, for you to optimize your energy and positive attitude, if you decorate your work environment in the pinky colours of the late dawn: golden pinks, salmon, mauve-pink. If you are going for an important interview, these colours would make a positive choice in your outfit, as they help you to project yourself in your most attractive and sensitive light.

WORK PROFILE
The 2 female boss

Serenely gliding through a field of chaos, feminine and **gracious** to the core, the **2** female directing her business team is a subtle **seductress** who entices everyone – both male and female – to give their best to the common cause. She is not aggressive or loud, but she **knows what she wants**, so don't mess with her system and think that she won't notice!

Everyone is fond of her, remembering her birthday and the scent she wears that makes the business space seem more human. She is **attentive** to the details her colleagues require, and is almost never high-handed unless some foolish underling underestimates her grip of matters. Just because she is **gentle**, she is not mindless of getting the job done. At her best in meetings where other peers are

2   3   4   5   6   7   8   9   1

trying to balance anger management and diplomacy, she finds **solutions** to everything from staffing issues to company image and profile, and she **listens** to what her team say with care and **sincerity**.

A good person to have on your side, the **2 female boss** has achieved her position through **genuine ability** and not through clever chat. Every detail concerns her, no matter how small, and she is **appreciative** of the contribution made by every person working with her. Her company will feel more like a **family business** than an impersonal work environment, and she fights for her workers like a **concerned parent**. And the ladies' room will be a pleasure to use, with beautiful products to enjoy as part of the norm. Just go and see ...

The 2 male boss

No less a **stickler** for standards and details than his female counterpart, the **2** male in charge of his group will be more like a **guiding** director and partner than a boss. He is **warm** and has a lovely humour, dresses with a surprising style, and has a way of speaking **appreciatively** to all the women he deals with in business without ever sounding condescending or inappropriately salacious.

He can be **charming** or fussy, but he uses his instincts all the time and is ahead of others in knowing what is right and wrong with his crew. He is probably more than ready to **muck in** with the freshest, most naive member of the business team to see how they are going and teach at **first hand**, and his ego is unlikely to get in the way of **good relations** between everyone. The office should feel

| 2 | 3 | 4 | 5 | 6 | 7 | 8 | 9 | 1 |

light and airy, and company celebrations or private birth-days will be remembered and handled with **aplomb**.

He is happier if there are other strong people in the firm, especially if some are women, with whom he has excellent rapport, and he has a **distinctive** way of getting things done. Many juniors get a chance to prove them-selves more quickly with a **2** at the helm, for – unafraid to **delegate** – no 2 boss of either sex has to have all the glory to themselves. This makes them **popular** with every-one, although they're **determined** to do a job well and are never the pushover they may appear to be to the uninitiated! If you work with – or for – a 2 male, don't try to get by with half-learned truths or uncertain facts. You'll find that you're embarrassed when he knows more about your job than you do.

The 2 female employee

Making her gentle and **accommodating** presence felt from the first, the **2** female employee slips into her work environment as though she's been there for months. She is the one who makes a point to remember colleagues' birthdays and names, and she immediately **distinguishes herself** with her feminine style and good taste, and her **willingness** to fit in and **learn** from everyone. Bossy co-workers think she'll be easy to push around, but discover at their peril that she can **stand her ground** and express herself with subtlety and **persuasiveness** – so don't take her on! Yet, if there is discord between other team members, she'll take it on herself to try to **smooth things along** and improve the overall dynamic – without expectation of thanks.

She's **fussy** about what tea she likes to drink, and what

2   3   4   5   6   7   8   9   1

cup she prefers to use, and if the ladies' room is messy or not aesthetically pleasing she will implement changes herself to make it better for all. She **floats** – rather than walks – around the office space, and has been talent-spotted because she is **capable** of an array of different things; yet she is **not strictly ambitious,** and rewards, when they come, will be an unexpected pleasure that delights her, rather than a just desert she was champing at the bit for. In short, she is the **near-perfect** employee, willing to do almost anything if it helps, and **kind** to others, too.

She is **well-organized**, and knows the answer – or will find out at once – if someone else doesn't, and carries an air of **youthfulness** that is pleasant for others to be around. Can she **annoy**? Yes. She won't tolerate anyone being unprepared for their day's job, or pretending they know something if they don't; nor will she excuse unnecessary rudeness – even from the boss. She may, therefore, **change the tone** over a period of time – but always for the better.

WORK PROFILE
The 2 male employee

Rather than watching his colleague's back to see how he can elbow his way into promotion in the first week, the **2** male employee **quietly** picks up the ways of the business world he has come into. **Listening** carefully, charming to those he works with, seemingly **gentle** but really very **astute**, he will quickly find his niche and **improve** the areas into which he is given input without a fanfare or much talk.

With excellent skills at **conciliation** and dealings with others, he will find himself **in demand** on many fronts, and covering a little bit of everything, although he is able to specialize, as well. As long as he is given plenty of **scope** without too much routine (for he is not a **4**!), he is happy to work as a member of a **cheerful** and spirited team,

| 2 | 3 | 4 | 5 | 6 | 7 | 8 | 9 | 1 |

THE 2 MALE EMPLOYEE

and never feels the pull to have the top job (although he will be delighted to be made a partner if the opening comes!). He is always thinking of what will be required to **facilitate** a job before it has been requested, and he is generally **amenable**, with a **calming influence** around him. Some may think him effeminate, though he is simply comfortable with his more **feminine side**, and he is able to wear pinks – shirts, ties or even a sweater – where other men fear venturing into this zone! His taste is **interesting** and varied, and he will be full of unusual suggestions about where to hold the office Christmas party or a celebratory lunch.

For anyone who fails to get close to this **diligent** and **responsive** individual, they may never know how clever and **sharp-witted** he is, since his appearance to the world is not 'carnivorous' so much as 'herbivorous'. But the **2** male employee has many strings to his bow, and is **nobody's fool**.

Ideal world or cruel world?
Best and worst jobs ...

IN AN IDEAL WORLD

Best job for a 2 female: Assistant to the head of the World Health Organization or the United Nations (diplomacy, detailed knowledge, doing something worthwhile, job creativity, being relied upon, no need for ego-stroking)

Best job for a 2 male: Partner in a media firm with varied communications and clients (buzz, challenge, liaison with associates, co-operative skills a premium)

IN A CRUEL WORLD

Worst job for a 2 female: Cataloguing a monastery's art collection/library with no scope for dealing with others/women (isolation, forced suppression of natural feminine charms)

Worst job for a 2 male: Personal assistant to a reclusive millionaire gentleman (no hope of breaking through the chilly persona, bored by solely male company!)

2   3   4   5   6   7   8   9   1

2'S CHILDHOOD

Seeing the way a number expresses itself in someone very young is fascinating, for the tendencies and responses are all in their infancy – and yet plain to see. Some facets of a number's power need to be grown into, and take time to reveal how they will be dealt with by the developing character. Sometimes the strength of a number can be a frustration when we're young.

If looking back on your own childhood through the lens of your number, you should discover – with considerable humour and irony – a renewed understanding of some of the difficulties or excitements you experienced. Or, if you have a child who is also a **2**, you may learn something more useful; it is an advantage to understand the qualities a number exudes over an awakening personality, especially in relation to talents and career strengths, as it might save a lot of frustrations. You'll be able to appreciate the positive traits, and handle negative ones more sympathetically.

Here, we take a detailed look at what it's like to be a child bearing your number. But what about the other numbers? Perhaps you have a child who is a **6**, and you'd like to know what that means? Or maybe you'd like to gain insight into friends' and siblings' childhoods, to see if it sheds any light on the people they have become today? A short profile is given for each number, along with advice for a **2** parent on dealing with other-number offspring.

Just as your own parents would have discovered when you yourself were a child, the hardest thing with a **2** child is dealing with their extreme sensitivity and their need to boost their self-confidence. **2**s are at their best with friends, and so a childhood that is too isolated or lacks company for them is a handicap.

A child born on the 2nd or the 20th is highly intuitive and subject to feelings of extreme sensitivity if they feel criticized. Intuitive and sometimes not always rational, these children have exceptional qualities of perception and feeling for others, and are particularly distressed by the suffering of both people and animals; it is not at all difficult to appeal to their deeply feeling natures. **2** children dream vividly, and take in acutely the visual details of life around them. Most importantly, they are unhappy if they are subjected to strife-riven domestic environments where the parents argue or resolve their differences through shouting!

2 children are quite content playing a supportive role towards their parents and friends, and they like company far better than playing alone – although if forced to be independent, they are often kept company by imaginary friends or playmates. If there is no tranquillity in a **2** child's environment, they can become disputatious and disruptive themselves, as their need for peace and a life of balance and harmony is very great. Loud noises and harsh words can almost make a **2** child physically sick, so try to be attentive to their need for gentleness from others. Because **2**s – even young **2**s – find co-operation naturally desirable, sibling rivalry is less of a problem with these children than many others; however, they are deeply affected if they feel another child is heeded or favoured unfairly.

A **2** child has a fine developing memory, and if you enhance their audio skills with radio programmes or talking books you will find they can be very entertaining, repeating what they have heard very precisely. This also appears in their musicality and, although **2** children are sometimes shy, they are surprisingly bold performers of whatever they feel a mastery over. Just as the adult **2** is known as the light-bearer to the world, your **2** child can be a developing

2's toys

Telephone • Walkie-talkie • Musical instrument • Ballet kit • Long skipping rope • Monopoly • Play make-up • Artist's equipment • Books • Membership to clubs

character bringing something intangible – a shining quality – to their family life; and they will also speak with a strength and wisdom beyond their age, at times. Encourage them to create and keep a haven of beauty in their personal world, for these habits will become building blocks upon which to found their future happiness and vocation.

The young master number 11

A child born on the 11th or the 29th of the month has a distinctive master-number personality, which becomes evident right from childhood. Just like the **2**s, **11** children

1   9   8   7   6   5   4   3   2

are highly sensitive and intuitive, but they are not quite as patient as **2**s, and feel the impetus to get on with things even in their earliest years. Moreover, **11** children are frustrated if they are treated as children, or if they are surrounded by others they see as immature or silly. This is a huge responsibility for a parent to deal with – dissuading a child from arrogance, and yet encouraging their excellence at the same time. It's quite a balancing act.

Children with this birthday exude a strange, otherworldly quality. At times their precocity is funny, at other times baffling, but they definitely see or understand things about this world that other children do not. Nevertheless, **11**s will take short cuts, if they can, to get on with what they see as being more important or interesting, and this penchant for abbreviating what is necessary to achieve in this life should – here and now – be discouraged.

As children (and in later life, if not handled carefully), **11**s are dreamers with grand ideas, some of which can astonishingly be brought to fruition, while others need a rational approach. **11**s live so much in their own landscape (or dreamscape) that they sometimes forget the real world, and this can cause unhappiness later in life, when no one quite measures up to their view of how it should be. On the other hand, these very visions are the stuff from which amazing new lands and worlds can be planned and created, and no one may do this more than a master-number child – whether **11** or even **22**. **11** children need time to consider what is important in life, and also to find their own philosophical truths – and neither do they come up with the banal answer they are always expected to. Their truths are based on different ideas of what is right or wrong.

Multi-talented and highly intelligent, they will want to make a splash in this world, so try to support their creativity and shape their minds without letting them get away with too much autonomy or selfishness. They need to live, at times, with others, to make the world a better place!

| 1 | 9 | 8 | 7 | 6 | 5 | 4 | 3 | 2 |

The 1 child

This resourceful child has a different way of thinking, and will stand to one side and evaluate things without pressure. Repeat Grandma's sound advice on any subject to a **1** under the age of six, and they'll simply ask, 'Why?' Ignoring the social expectation to conform, **1** children often make us laugh with surprise.

A **1** child is tough and active – an inquisitive soul who wants to get on with things and not be held in check by others, however wise the parental eye might be. Stubborn and impatient, **1**s frequently suffer by questioning – though not from rudeness – the authority of a parent or teacher. **1**s break down tradition and find new ideas to form a fresh understanding of the world we're in. Your **1** child needs careful handling: a bright mind bursting with interest and disinclined to authority needs subtle direction

— for which a patient, loving **2** parent is ideally suited. If **1** children dominate their friends and talk over their family, it can make them socially inept and unable to co-operate in love relationships later in life, leading to loneliness rather than just self-reliance.

A **1**'s greatest challenge is to learn to live in a social world and understand that they are not inevitably right. To foster a **1**'s unique personality and avoid insensitivity to others, let them behave like an adult. This confidence a **1** child will ably repay. **1** children suffer from being misunderstood, as they're often so happy in their private hours and so demanding of having their own time that they may not learn to express their need for others. The seeds are sown early as to how to approach another person for signs of affection, and a sensitive **2** parent might simply wade in across the private moat and cover their **1** child with kisses when the time seems to demand it. **1**s need just such an intuitive parent as you!

The 3 child

From the cradle, **3**s hold parties and like to mix with other children. They have a capacity to laugh and precipitate laughter, even when things go a little wrong. **3** children are like the reappearing sun after rain, and their energies can be restorative for everyone. Creative and playful, nothing keeps them low for long.

Like a juggler keeping plates and balls in the air, **3**s have several activities and talents on the go from the start. This can be a problem, however: making decisions is hard for them, and they need a wise older counsellor who can talk out the options and give them room to think. Even then, a decision once reached can always be changed – and a **3** child will find a way to run in several directions at one time.

Keep your **3** busy with lots of artistic activities, using colours and textures – right from babyhood – to open their eyes to what they can do. Even before the age of ten, a strong personal taste will begin to develop – and it may not be the same as their parents'. Using up their flow of energy on a multitude of tasks will be demanding on both parents, but the 3 child does give a great deal back in return.

3s are talkers and have a witty repartee, even when tiny: you'll be surprised at what you hear from them sometimes, and will wonder where it came from. Naturally gifted at PR, they will talk you around when you are set against one of their wishes, but you will need to direct them now and again or nothing will ever be finished! A 2 parent with a 3 child should give them freedom to experiment, and not be upset if they are sometimes messy or chatter too much. Be loving and kind, and don't worry if they rush about without your serenity: they have a way of coming back smiling.

1 9 8 7 6 5 4 3 2

The 4 child

Surprisingly insecure and in need of praise, these children are reliable and hard-working and want to do well. They are their own worst critics at times, second only to number **7** children, and they glow when appreciated. They are happiest with family around them – even extended members – and often prefer holidays in familiar places. That said, they can be very quiet and self-sufficient when required, for they concentrate well.

These are organized children who won't cope well if their parents aren't as organized as they are! Never lose a school form or an item from their games kit on a crucial day, as this will cause them serious panic. They like to have material possessions around them because this bolsters their feeling of security, and will manage their pocket money well, content to do odd jobs and chores to gain this reward.

| 2 | 3 | 4 | 5 | 6 | 7 | 8 | 9 | 1 |

4s love the earth and buildings. They will treasure a patch of garden given them to tend, or a garden house they can extend or build outright. If they are born on the 22nd, rather than the 4th, 13th or 31st, they will truly have architectural talents, and may follow design as a career later. All **4** children, though, are handy at craft work and excellent at projects which require intelligence combined with method to get something done. They hate being late and don't admire tardiness in others, either.

As children, **4**s are loyal and dependable to family and friends, and are more patient than many numbers. They will make light of complex tasks, but they need to be allowed to do things in their own way. A **2** parent will appreciate a **4** child's care and order, even if they seem, perhaps, slightly unimaginative; they simply have a different approach to the duties of life. **4**s – like you – feel more responsible towards others, which **2**s will encourage. This is a good co-operative number for you, and the relationship should prosper.

1   9   8   7   6   5   4   3   2

The 5 child

Unable to be confined or to sit still, a **5** child is bursting with curiosity about life and people. Very sociable and happy to be on the move, these adventurous youngsters have much in common with **1**s, but are more willing to work in a team, and good at picking up on other people's ideas, only to improve them.

From their first few words, **5** children have good memories and a facility for speech – they speak and learn quickly, and can pick up more than one language. Even more physical than **1**s (although the two numbers are alike in this), they are excellent at sport or physical co-ordination. They chatter, are full of energy, and like to play to an audience. But most importantly, **5** children love to be free – to explore, laze, hunt, create, discover and travel. Take your **5** child away on holiday and they quickly make friends with

| 2 | 3 | 4 | 5 | 6 | 7 | 8 | 9 | 1 |

others, and acquire a taste for foreign places. They will even experiment with different food, if you're lucky.

5s find a reason to slip away if they're bored with adult company – so don't be offended. Their minds can pursue several streams of active interest, so they need a great deal of amusement to stretch them. This adventurous spirit can be a worry to their family sometimes and, indeed, 5s need to understand house rules about asking first, or telling someone where they're off to. The difficulty is that 5 children usually don't want to explain themselves to anyone.

The test for a 5's parent is to set their child constructive challenges that will vent their curiosity in good ways. 5s will pick up technology and music (other forms of language, in a sense) quickly, but they don't like dull routine work – which will irritate a 4 sibling if they have one. A 2 parent of a 5 should be patient with their clever, restless offspring, as they are quick on the uptake, but arguments about their freedom to roam may be a problem.

1 9 8 7 6 5 4 3 2

The 6 child

With many similarities to **2**, here is a young soul in need of a peaceful haven; a **6** will feel ill if there is dissension around them. Always wanting to beautify their surroundings and make pretty presents for Mum, these talented, sensitive children have many gifts for creative expression. They will also nurse the sick cat or anyone who needs gentle kindness, but are not always robust themselves, and should be sheltered from bad weather or aggressive viruses.

As children, **6**'s musical talents should emerge – and they often have beautiful speaking or singing voices. They are also the peacemakers of the family – natural creators of balance and harmony. Give them a free hand with their bedroom and their flower garden, and be ready to learn from them. Both boys and girls usually make good cooks when they are older, too, so time spent in the kitchen won't

2   3   4   5   6   7   8   9   1

be wasted. Birthday presents that foster their good eye — a camera or set of art tools — will usually fit them well.

Despite being sensitive to others and quite intuitive, **6** as a child is a little shy and needs drawing out — especially if there has been much change in their young life, because **6** children need stability and like to remain a tiny bit traditional. They become very attached to their home. But if their family life is unconventional they will ultimately adjust, because they offer their family a lot of love, and like to be shown love in return. Even the boys have a feminine side, which in no way calls their gender into question.

Good at school and almost as well-organized as **4**s, this is a number which needs time to grow into itself: **6**s really are enormously talented. A **2** parent will always be gentle with a **6** child, who is artistic and sensitive in so many similar ways. When you need a friend to listen, support, encourage and back *you* up, you will often find unsuspected reservoirs of strength in this interesting child.

| 1 | 9 | 8 | 7 | 6 | 5 | 4 | 3 | 2 |

The 7 child

Even in primary school this is a child with a focused mind and a strongly developed critical sense. A **7** child is perceptive and, sometimes, disarmingly quiet. They will often prefer adult company, as their peers will probably seem too young and underdeveloped to them. Wise and difficult to know well, these are children with a serious cast to their intelligent minds.

The fact that a **7** child can sit quietly and contemplate things deeply should not imply that they are introverted: quite the opposite. A **7** will grow into a very good host as long as the company appeals, and they have a lovely sense of humour, apparent from their earliest years – even if it does sometimes find expression at others' expense. They will rarely be rude, but certainly have a good understanding of all that has been said – and what has not been.

| 2 | 3 | 4 | 5 | 6 | 7 | 8 | 9 | 1 |

Listen to their impressions of the people they deal with!

All **7**s as children have an inward reluctance to accept other people's ideas automatically – rather like **1**s – but there is a special propensity to independence in a child born on the 16th. This is the number of someone who finds it difficult asking for what they want – someone who often feels as though they haven't been consulted as to their own wishes. And all **7**s certainly have definite ideas about what to believe.

7 children should be told the truth on virtually all matters; they will know if they are being deceived, and will respect being treated as an adult in any case. A **2** parent understands this intuitively, and respects their **7** child's strength. Though different – a **7** child keen to retire into privacy and personal space – these two numbers understand each other fairly well, and a **7** child gives you much to be proud of, both academically and in terms of humanitarian feelings.

1   9   8   7   6   5   4   3   2

The 8 child

Here we have a young executive in the making. Even when they are still at school these children have a canny nose for what will make good business – and yet they are generous, hard-working and prepared to learn everything it will take to succeed in this life. Children born on the 8th, 17th and 26th like to have charge of their own finances, and to be given scope to do 'grown-up' activities – organizing their own parties and making arrangements for outings with their friends.

These children have strength and energy, but mentally are reflective and wise, too. They always see both sides to an argument – so parents who ask them to choose sides, beware! An **8** makes good judgements, and even before the age of ten they have a sense of what is fair and what is morally right.

| 2 | 3 | 4 | 5 | 6 | 7 | 8 | 9 | 1 |

As this number rules the octave, many **8** children are extremely musical and have a wonderful sense of rhythm. This last even assures they can be good at sport, as it takes innate timing to perfect many physical skills. **8**s also like philosophical ideas and relish being given 'big concepts' to chew over, especially concerning politics or religious ideas. **8**s are proud, and like to research things carefully – so as long as they are not bored, you will find an **8** child with their head in a book or on the internet, or watching programmes that educate and broaden their vistas.

Rather like you, an **8** child is always striving for balance, and this will help you to be pragmatic if they are sometimes pulling in the opposite direction from you. **8**s are loyal to those they love, but a delicate sensibility makes them look at the other side of a story, or fight for an underdog. You understand this urge very well, and mostly you will respect the qualities and mind of your generous **8** child.

1   9   8   7   6   5   4   3   2

The 9 child

Here is a person born for the theatre, or to travel the world and befriend everyone. **9**s have an expansive view of things, and don't like to be restricted. With a good head for both science and the arts, there are many career directions a **9** may take, so parents will have their work cut out trying to help them choose. However, because the number **9** is like a mirror, with every number added to it reducing again to that same number (for example: 5+9 = 14, and 1+4 = 5), **9** children are able to take on the feelings of just about anyone, which is why they are so artistic and good at drama and writing.

From their first years in school it will be clear a **9** child has a wonderful dry sense of humour and a taste for the unusual. **9** children are not often prejudiced and seem to be easy-going – though they are sensitive to the atmos-

2   3   4   5   6   7   8   9   1

phere around them, picking up vibes like a sponge. If you speak to them harshly they will take it seriously, and are protective of others who seem to be hurt in this way too.

9s have a delicate relationship with their parents, but particularly with the father figure. A **9** girl will want to idolize her dad, and will feel desperately disappointed if circumstances are against this, while a **9** boy may wish to emulate his father – and yet they often grow up without enough input from this important person, who is busy or away. A **9** child must be wise ahead of their time, and so this lesson is thrown at them in one guise or another.

The **2** parent of a **9** child must go with the flow, allowing a stream of friends and interests through their door! Your **9** child appreciates your sensitivity, and equally recognizes your need to be kept in the picture, and will reward you with affection and kindness. Grown-ups from the start, your **9** child's philosophical mind and willingness to keep the peace fill you with admiration.

1   9   8   7   6   5   4   3   2

2 AT PLAY

We have discovered how your number expresses itself through your character in relation to your family and your general personality, what instinctive reactions go with your number in everyday situations, and how it might shape your career path and colour your childhood. But every day our DAY number also influences the way we respond to the social world around us. So, what can it say about our leisure hours? Is yours a number that even allows itself to relax? (Well, you probably already have some answers to this one!) What can your number reveal about the way you like to spend your time, or how you achieve pleasure outside of duty?

2 3 4 5 6 7 8 9 1

Over the next few pages we take a look at what makes you tick, as a **2** (or **11**), when you are unwinding – and how **2**s prefer to fill their time, if given a choice. Let's see whether you're typical in this respect ... And who knows – if you haven't already tried all the activities and pastimes mentioned, maybe you'll get a few ideas about what to put on your list for next time!

The 2 woman at play

With all that you have read to this point, you know that your ideal world offers you a balance between 'people time' and 'unwinding time', and that creating sanctuary is a priority. When you choose how to spend your leisure hours, you like to achieve a harmony between these needs – of having friends and loved ones nearby, and of relaxing in a peaceful space. Much of your creativity is prompted by this balance, too.

And leisure, for you, often does mean 'people time'. If your career keeps you on your toes, your hours off will be happiest if they are spent close to your lover and your family. Walking and talking without rushing, or dining out with time to talk, have a strong appeal, and your natural enjoyment of food and company makes you – like **6**s – very happy to play hostess to friends and achieve the perfect backdrop to a gathering, with beautiful music and decoration. You love doing things for others, and you love their reaction. Your intuition also lets you to know when someone needs some quality time with you, and you make this a pleasure in your free time rather than a burden of responsibility.

2 women would regard a long weekend — or week away — at a spa retreat as pure bliss. Enjoying all the care and attention someone else has put into the décor and the treatments offered, you will also find that the experience of unwinding in this way prompts your meditative/creative powers. You rightly see a touch of self-pampering as justified — just because it does indeed give you this crucial thinking time, and allow you to listen to whoever you are with.

It is no surprise to find **2**s at home preparing for weekend guests, attending to every detail, and your free time is often an excuse to try out new ideas. In an ideal world

1   9   8   7   6   5   4   3   2

your home will be big enough to give you a proper guest room in which to indulge anyone who comes to you for that spa therapy; but even if your chance to play host only runs to a pretty sofa bed and a vase of flowers beside it, no one other than a **6** will take greater trouble than you do. You are especially adept at creating a romantic hideaway for friends and relatives, and you do think of everything. You will also take the trouble to hand-make any number of items to add luxury.

Designing your own clothes, dancing away the late hours and reading peacefully all have individual appeal at appropriate times. But your real creative flair emerges when you design a romantic weekend for the person in your heart. You will dream up treats and surprises, think of sensuous indulgences, and make no complaint if you spend literally hours researching options with a travel agent or on the internet. Details are your speciality, and no one will do the job of planning and executing as well as you. Thus, one of your favourite personal leisure treats will be perfecting the weekend away; and you may cast your net far and wide.

There will never be enough time in life for a **2** woman to perfect her many gifts, but learning more about any 'feminine' skills – from piano playing and flamenco dancing, to flower arranging, tapestry making or cake baking – will inspire your private hours. When you relax you are happiest doing something gentle, as time-wasting is not your preferred thing. Taking the trouble to add finishing touches to your home or garden will be as much a treat in a week off as sorting out your drawers can be when you have a sudden free day.

The 2 man at play

Though many will never know it, the gentle **2** man is quite comfortable spending his free time doing some rather thrilling things. He is as likely as a **1** man to enjoy speed on the road or – more likely still – on the water, and he is perfectly ready to try any other outdoor physical activity ... but with one huge difference. The **2** man likes to take his partner along.

Just like **2** women, you'll try your hand at a vast number of leisure activities which are specially geared for **2** people. The romantic side of your nature will research the best moonlit beach on which to walk with your lover – and, equally, give cycling through France a try with your perfect soulmate. And if you have children, they will be strapped into baby slings or child seats, and taken too. You love to spend your leisure time with those in your personal life.

2 3 4 5 6 7 8 9 1

2 men surprise the rest of us with the scope of their interest. You may be attracted to archaeology, fine art or cookery, and could also be a brilliant sketcher or musician. Any unwinding time which allows the space to develop these talents is going to be a plus. And **2** men usually have a talent for sports too, as their basic gifts derive in part from a great sense of rhythm. If a **1** likes to rifle-shoot or bungee jump, a **2** perhaps prefers tennis with a partner, or squash, or even croquet. Competition is less an issue than companionship and good sportsmanship.

Just as with a female **2**, a **2** male is perfectly at home (and not ashamed of it!) in a spa. You will appreciate unwinding in a tranquil atmosphere with delicious smells and softly spoken attendants, and will quite possibly be an aficionado of the many treatments and therapies on offer. You may be quite proud of your hands, and keep them immaculately clean and well-manicured, and your physical appearance will receive almost as much attention as a female **2**'s. For any woman looking for a partner in retail therapy, a patient **2** man is happy to spend his free hours shopping for fashion and food, and will be almost as comfortable with whisks and saucepans as a **6** man: both are talented and generous chefs. A cookery holiday will appeal to a male **2**, especially if he is treated to a tranquil location in which to hone his skills.

2s love the water, so holidays and days off which take you to the sea or out boating will have a double impact of reviving your soul and prompting your romantic nature. And if a garden project at home includes putting in a pond or a water feature, you are likely to be more than willing to give up other activities to do a garden makeover.

2 is a romantic number and, as a **2** man, you will enjoy being invited by your partner to be sensuous and loving in a pretty place on a free day. Your mood will be affected by the atmosphere and aesthetic experience, however, so your partner will need to bear this in mind, and take time to get this right – and they will be rewarded by a very loving and sexy partner to pamper them in return. Things will usually only stale if work denies you the leisure time to indulge: if your partner prioritizes this one-on-one holiday time, this will keep the romance alive – and if they take the trouble to create surprises and organize these details, you will find ways to show your appreciation!

Others shouldn't underestimate how daring you can be: you may prefer a more private audience, but you are full of fun and humour, and unexpected eccentricities. And, if your partner responds approvingly, there is no end to the variety of ways to spend your free hours together – something that goes hand in hand with a relationship with a male **2**. You're also a good listener, and will be very willing to give your partner your full attention, as long as the environment is supportive of gentleness and quiet conversation. In fact, you're a perfect partner to do almost anything with, really.

1 9 8 7 6 5 4 3 2

2 IN LOVE

Love: it's what we all want to know about.
What's your style as a lover? And your taste –
where does that run? Do you want a partner who
is, ideally, as independent as you? Or would you
rather have a love in your life who is happy to
take the lead and let you follow along, to share in
their discoveries at your own pace? Everything
about you screams 'partnership', but is this
all there is to your love life?

Our first task is to consider how you see others as potential partners, and what you are likely to need from them.
Why are you attracted to someone in the first place? This
is where we begin ... But then you might like to pass the
book across to your other half (if you have one), for the

2   3   4   5   6   7   8   9   1

second subject of discussion is: why are *they* attracted to *you*? What does it mean to have a **2** lover?

Telltale traits of the 2 lover
- Accommodating, affectionate, idealistic
- Believes in partner
- Gentle humour with surprising subtlety which catches others unaware
- Sensuous, rather than brazenly sexy
- Romantic – loves to be pampered
- Not likely to want (or need) scores of lovers – ready to settle for the right one
- Stylish dresser

1 9 8 7 6 5 4 3 2

How do you do?
A 2 IN ATTRACTION

Whether you're a man or woman, still young or settling comfortably into middle age, you are romantic in your expectations about relationships, and may never feel absolutely complete unless you have a partner to share life with. The most giving and naturally co-operative number of all, you are a delightful partner for anyone who is willing to take you seriously, but you need loyalty from the person you're attracted to very early on, and this influences your style in getting to know someone right from the first.

Easily flirtatious without being aggressive, you have a true charm which draws the opposite sex smoothly, and allows you plenty of choice as to who you will let get closer to you. But you are fussy about the one you love, and you set very high standards for another person to live

2   3   4   5   6   7   8   9   1

up to. You must look up to the one you will spend time with and, as someone who is not unhappy to follow rather than lead, you need to put your weight behind a person you respect. You don't like flashy or vulgar lovers, but you do like someone who is distinctive and seems assured of where they're going. You will also prefer a partner who has considerable style!

That special someone ...

You will give endlessly once you have pledged your heart, and you expect something special for this degree of commitment. You have a strong desire for companionship from your love, so you need to be with someone who is a joy to listen to — for listen you will. Moreover, love has a poetic appeal for you, and you will rarely under-sell yourself, which means the love you choose must offer you something unique. You would love to find the partner who will write

1   9   8   7   6   5   4   3   2

you love songs or paint you a picture, design you a garden or stage perfect scenarios for two, to go nearly anywhere together. And you like a partner with a brain, who you can get behind and promote gently to the world.

You are the most generous lover, never needing to be in the limelight but delighted when you feel truly appreciated – which is, perhaps, a role that only a civilized and well-mannered human being can respect fully. If you are with anyone who is a taker, selfish and arrogant, you will become disillusioned and unhappy, and feel – quite fairly – that you have been taken for granted. It is a special soul who will not abuse your gentleness or conciliatory nature, who must be your perfect match. Of course, this doesn't necessarily reflect the way things are in the ordinary world of human beings!

Always willing to make concessions to your loved one, you may appear indecisive in relationships. In fact, you know what you want but you have to be careful of misplaced trust in others. If you experience many domestic upsets or changes in your early life, you will place even greater emphasis on finding the perfect relationship. You have a dream of what you want and, being so deeply affectionate, you may be a victim of depression when others cannot express themselves as you would like. And if your loved one proves faithless or inconstant, you can go into a serious decline. For this reason, try to place your affections carefully, and don't let yourself build illusions over human beings.

Hidden strengths

For all this dreamy idealistic hope, however, you are interesting when it comes to relationships, for although **2** is a number that prides itself on flexibility, in relationships it has astonishing strengths. You are able to make changes without being weak, and you have, in fact, a very strong character when it comes to loving – especially if you are an **11** variant of **2**. This enables you to attract an interesting mate – someone who is aware of your extraordinariness. Not everyone will appreciate your sensitive nature and intuitive essence of being, but the one who does will indeed be a special person too.

And what are you likely to want in a partner? Strangely, although you like beautiful things and will be happier if your life is not too stretched financially, you are not at all concerned with what you may call *superficialities*. Vanity, riches, fame, jealousy, ego are all the luxuries of life that might seem desperately important to many, but for you they hold little illusion. You would rather have a love who is a person of substance, without these frivolities, for you are aware that happiness is not in material things. What is of real value to you, rather, is character and courage, and you will wish for – and be with – someone whom you see embodying just those qualities.

To have and to hold?

LOVING A NUMBER 2

If you are in love with a **2**, you have chosen a deeply loving partner who has seen something very special in you. **2** is not attracted by flashiness, or by boastful individuals who are in a social race of keeping up with any Joneses! **2**s love a partner who has tender merits – a gentle troubadour spirit, perhaps, and a kind word for others in the world. You will always feel the pressure not to let them down; and, sometimes, **2**'s naivety will seem unbelievable. But a gentle **2** lover – given a chance – wants to believe the best about people, and you will be amazed sometimes at how this faith in others is strangely repaid to a **2**.

You may be fascinated by your **2**'s ability to shine softly at social gatherings – a knack they have for pouring forth an inner light without having to try to be drop-dead

1 9 8 7 6 5 4 3 2

arresting to a crowd. **2**'s magnetic quality is like a good perfume – designed to be savoured by those nearest, rather
than brash enough to warn others they're coming from a
mile away. And, like a good wine, **2**'s talents and strengths
grow from year to year, as they acquire more confidence in
the hands of a good lover. Look after your **2**, and you'll have
a partner to see you through the very long race that is life.

Feminine charms

So what drew you to this person in the first place? If you
are a man, you were attracted to your partner's femininity
conjoined with grace and insight about the world; her
mind, her appetites and her excellent taste are envied by
many friends. Or, if you are a woman, you no doubt admire
your male **2**'s *difference* – his being comfortable with his
feminine side, able to cook and discuss literature that is
supposed to be written for women, or possibly even his

being able to cry at a good movie, or if a friend is in trouble, or a child in pain. Either way, your **2** lets their feelings show without apology.

And they are rhythmic, of course, good lovers, able to offer you a surrounding feeling of peace and calm after a difficult day. Artistic and sensitive, they are prepared to listen attentively to what you say. To appreciate the charms of a **2** is to recognize the claims of a classic car – a Bentley, perhaps, or, in today's world, an Audi cabriolet – in preference to a brasher Maserati or an obvious Porsche. Your **2** is never loud, always alluring and a riddle to know. Like the moon, a **2** lover has phases – bubbly and adventurous, fragile and insecure. This is partly what draws you.

And the drawbacks?

On down days, loving a **2** can be frustrating. If an extreme lack of confidence shadows their moves, they can be afraid to make decisions or rest with any peace. A **2** without inner peace is a travesty. Or, if they are over-sensitive (often a difficulty), you may feel stifled by your **2**, or irritated by their inability to get angry when they should actually do so. Instead, a thwarted **2** will grumble and go into their shell, and the rest of life may pass along without them understanding where a fairy-tale went wrong, or why they proved too cloying for a lover they believed they were merely supporting and reassuring. If a **2** is out of balance emotionally, it can be suffocating, or seem like you have to make all the moves and come up with all of the plans. Or, possibly, your **2** is too easily depressed if there is the smallest thing out of sorts in the home.

For the most part, though, your **2** wants to settle any disagreements amicably, and has a powerful, intelligent subconscious mind that can be a reservoir of real strength for you, and all those close to you both, in times of trouble. A **2**'s essence is quite magical – being the ultimate expression of the best that is female – and they have a direct line to the memory that is the universe. This certainly makes a fascinating partner – one who will give, and find new ways of giving, and who will be a pleasing friend and tasteful but exciting lover. Romantic imagination is rarely in short supply for a **2**, and you have chosen someone to love who is in danger only of being placed too high upon a pedestal, or doing the same with you. Tread softly!

2 in love

Turn-ons:

- ♥ ✔ A sensuous lover who is energetic and takes romantic chances
- ♥ ✔ Someone who loves to unwind in unhurried seclusion, one on one
- ♥ ✔ A lovely, melodic speaking voice
- ♥ ✔ Someone who smells clean!

Turn-offs:

- ♥ ✗ An arrogant partner who treats you like their private secretary – without saying 'thank you'!
- ♥ ✗ Someone with sloppy habits (especially in the bedroom)
- ♥ ✗ Someone who fails to notice the fresh flowers and beautiful clean sheets
- ♥ ✗ Anyone who only talks about themselves

2 3 4 5 6 7 8 9 1

2'S COMPATIBILITY

In this weighty section you have the tools to find
out how well you click with all the other numbers
in matters of the heart, but also when you have to
work or play together too. Each category opens with
a star-ratings chart, showing you – at a glance –
whether you're going to encounter plain sailing or
stormy waters in any given relationship. First up is
love: if your number matches up especially well with
the person you're with, you will appreciate why
certain facets of your bond just seem to slot
together easily.

But, of course, we're not always attracted to the people
who make the easiest relationships for us, and if you find
that the one you love rates only one or two stars, don't

1   9   8   7   6   5   4   3   2

give in! Challenges are often the 'meat' of a love affair — and all difficulties are somewhat soothed if you both share a birthday number in common, even if that number is derived from the *total* of the birth date rather than the actual DAY number. In other words, if your partner's LIFE number is the same as your DAY number, you will feel a pull towards each other which is very strong, even if the DAY numbers taken together have some wrinkles in their match-up. You will read more about this in the pages that follow the star chart.

The charts also include the master numbers **11** and **22**: these bring an extra dimension to relationships for those whose birth-number calculations feature either of these numbers at any stage. (For example, someone with a DAY number of **4** may be born on the 22nd: 2+2 = **4**. This means you should read the compatibility pairings for your number with both a **4** and a **22**.)

Sometimes the tensions that come to the surface in

love relationships are excellent for business relationships instead: the competitiveness that can undermine personal ties can accelerate effectiveness in working situations. We'll take a look at how other numbers match up with yours in vocational situations. And, when it comes to friends, you'll see why not all of your friendships are necessarily a smooth ride ...

In all matters — whether love, work or friendship — you will probably discover that the best partnerships you make involve an overlap of at least one number that you share in common. A number **2** attracts other number **2**s in various close ties throughout life.

NOTE: To satisfy your curiosity, ALL numbers are included in the star charts, so that you can check the compatibility ratings between your friends, co-workers and loved ones — and see why some relationships may be more turbulent than others!

| 1 | 9 | 8 | 7 | 6 | 5 | 4 | 3 | 2 |

Love

YOUR **LOVE** COMPATIBILITY CHART

	1	2	3	4	5
With a 1	★★★★	★★★★★	★★	★★★	★★★★★
With a 2	★★★★★	★★★★	★★★	★★★★★	★
With a 3	★★	★★★	★★★★★	★★	★★★★
With a 4	★★★	★★★★★	★★	★★★★	★★
With a 5	★★★★★	★	★★★★	★★	★★★
With a 6	★★★	★★★★	★★★★	★★★	★★
With a 7	★★★★★	★★	★★★	★★★★★	★★★
With an 8	★★★★	★★★★	★★★★★	★★★	★★★
With a 9	★★★	★★★	★★★★★	★★	★★★
With an 11	★★★★	★★★★	★★	★★★★★	★★
With a 22	★★★★	★★★★★	★★★	★★★★	★★★★

2   3   4   5   6   7   8   9   1

6	7	8	9	11	22
★★★	★★★★★	★★★★	★★★	★★★★	★★★★
★★★★	★★	★★★★	★★★	★★★★	★★★★★
★★★★	★★★	★★★★★	★★★★★	★★	★★★
★★★	★★★★★	★★★	★★	★★★★★	★★★★
★★	★★★	★★★	★★★	★★	★★★★
★★★★★	★	★★★	★★★★★	★★★★	★★★★
★	★★★	★★★★	★★★	★★★★	★★★★★
★★★	★★★★	★★★	★★	★★★★★	★★★★
★★★★★	★★★	★★	★★★	★★★★	★★★
★★★★	★★★★	★★★★★	★★★★	★★	★★★★★
★★★★	★★★★★	★★★★	★★★	★★★★★	★★

1 9 8 7 6 5 4 3 2

2 in love with a 1   ★★★★★

You two are naturally drawn to each other, because **1** is a leader and **2** is always ready to follow what is interesting and seems right. A **1** has a true appreciation for the aesthetic beauty you exude as a **2**, and will love the gentle and pretty domestic environment **2** is able to provide. In fact, **2** offers peace, which is often a real respite from the battles **1** takes on in the big wide world, and this haven also gives you both the necessary breathing space to think up clever ideas and create projects together on a large scale.

Most importantly, **2** believes in clever **1**. You know they have great plans, and that you're heading somewhere, and, while your **1** is impatient and in a rush to get on, you are less frantic, and find a way to help your partner execute some very original ideas. Your sensitive and highly intuitive spirit recognizes **1**'s talents and takes pride in them. **1**'s

| 2 | 3 | 4 | 5 | 6 | 7 | 8 | 9 | 1 |

LOVE

leadership qualities are very different from your wish to shore up your partner's insecurities, and readiness to be the unsung hero. Luckily for 1, 2 has the tact and discretion to smooth over the ruffled feathers 1s can sometimes create by being over-enthusiastic or irritated by conservative thinking. 2 knows when 1 is right, but has the political acumen to put things to the other concerned parties. You understand instinctively how to support your 1's talents and make sure they come before the right audience.

Being utterly feminine and completely charming – even if you are the male partner! – you bring out the male energy and determination in your number 1 partner better than anybody else. Where 1 is innovative, 2 follows through for them; and when your 1 has a (not infrequent) need for privacy, you are unoffended and help to create that space, defending your 1 even against their own family. 2 knows 1's bark is usually worse than their bite, even if others are not so sure!

1   9   8   7   6   5   4   3   2

A **2** loving a **1** is one of the best pairings in numerology, because these numbers fit together like night and day. Perhaps no one else will give **1** as much faith and put as much energy into their dreams as **2** will; and, possibly, no one inspires a **2** more than a **1** can. But there is a difficulty. Sometimes **2**s give the impression of being so compliant that they are weak, and this is not so. You can be stubborn and easily offended, so your often impetuous **1** would do well to remember that the words they say will bruise if they are cruel, and really leave a mark on your gentle nature, whereas other numbers will know not to pay too close attention to the unintended insult — or perhaps have a higher view of themselves. As a **2**, you are so willing to give **1** the lead that they may abuse this at times, and fail to notice your contribution to their success. Your **1** shines because, partly, you help them to; and you must gently remind your charismatic **1** not to dominate your surprisingly strong and sensitive soul.

| 2 | 3 | 4 | 5 | 6 | 7 | 8 | 9 | 1 |

2 has a lot of the qualities **1** lacks – of being conscious of how others are feeling, of knowing when to back off for a while, of being happy not to be in the forefront. You can hug your **1** without them asking, because you know – without being told – that your independent-seeming **1** needs it. And **1** has the dynamism and spirit to lift you out of any kind of commonplace or lacklustre life; you aren't pushy, and often settle for less than perfection from the world around you, just for the sake of tranquillity. **1** has what it takes to stand up and fight your battles when you can't, along with their own. And no one will sing your praises louder.

Key themes

You beautify the space you live in together • Share strong likes and dislikes • Balance of feminine and masculine energy • Inventive sensual relationship, as **2** is a very giving and generous lover

| 1 | 9 | 8 | 7 | 6 | 5 | 4 | 3 | 2 |

2 in love with a 2   ★★★★

2s together in a relationship may not shake the world or come up with a cure for cancer, but this is a relationship of real feeling and quality. Better would be if one of you were an **11** (*see page 172*), so that there would be a natural partner taking the lead or shouldering the burdens; however, even two pure **2**s have a chance for serious happiness together.

You share a desire for peace and equilibrium, with an innate understanding of each other's fears, joys, vulnerabilities and pleasures. And you share well, knowing how to meet each other halfway emotionally. Subtleties abound between you, in the way you communicate and the needs you translate to one another. There is nothing brash or crass about **2**s in a close relationship.

One of the best aspects of this pairing is that the bond

| 2 | 3 | 4 | 5 | 6 | 7 | 8 | 9 | 1 |

grows stronger and more flexible over time, once a level of trust has been established. Every time lovers come together with one number in common – it may be the **DAY** number and the **LIFE** number, as well – there is a feeling of familiarity, of having known each other before, and this is especially true for intuitive **2**s. There may be frequent occurrences of déjà vu between you, or of sharing a dream consciousness, and it is certainly the case that you can often read each other without the need for language. You have a deep understanding of one another, and you build on your relationship over the years so that a greater feeling of friendship and loyalty comes to replace initial physical attraction – although the sensual element of the relationship will remain strong.

The most effective way to organize this relationship is for you to discover ways of working with one another to achieve goals and dreams, rather than one of you trying – perhaps ineffectively – to dominate the other. Partnership is natural and desirable for both lovers, and this should be a starting point: playing games or feigning independence will be a waste of time and confuse one (or both) of you. There is a chance, however, that being too aware of each other's sensitivities may constrict you from honesty – that you both make unnecessary sacrifices, rather than admit to each other what you need. Also, **2**s together can be very indecisive, and find it hard to make definite steps towards your goals. But if you can share these needs, and give each other room to specialize in different aspects of the relationship, this partnership should grow into a strong and healthy tree that flourishes in a loving garden. You will surely share an aesthetically uplifting home and have many friends.

Children are important in the lives of two **2** parents, and you will be excellent guides and very sensitive to their needs. There could be a small danger of expecting a great deal from them, because you are somewhat perfectionist yourselves – only slightly less so than number **7**. Two **2**s, therefore, will ask a lot of each other together – and of their family, wanting good school results and excellent manners socially. There is also a possibility that you will be too idealistic together, as **2** is a number that always expects a perfect partner, and doubling this will exacerbate this desire. Overall, though, this is a very good relationship, and should last many years, altering its focus and momentum over time.

Key themes

Tacit agreement to share burdens and decisions • Thinking as one • Priority of establishing a tranquil space together, and a beautiful home and garden • May have to fight against becoming too unadventurous, and getting into habits rather than trying new things

1   9   8   7   6   5   4   3   2

2 in love with a 3   ★★★

These two numbers are attracted to each other physically – very much so. **3** has an energy and vitality that appeals to tranquil **2**, being so different from **2**'s own love of gentleness and quietude. **3** seems so sparky and confident, so alluring and young at heart, while **2** seems – to **3** – so still and serene, so grown up and caring towards other people. And **3** is definitely attracted by **2**'s physical beauty and good taste – even though it is not their own kind of taste. So, the sexual tension is likely to be sizzling for a while – but only for a while! After some time passes, problems will inevitably settle in ...

These two numbers have very different expectations of life, and different energies. It is not beyond possibility that this relationship could work – partly because the attraction is so strong. But difficulties arise in the day-to-

2   3   4   5   6   7   8   9   1

day harmony. **3** is likely to feel that you are too staid and conservative in your whole approach to life, while you may feel (with some justification!) that **3** is lacking inner focus and seriousness about life. **3** may seem, by twists and turns, both marvellously free of social constraint and ridiculously immature. When things are fine, it will be the former, but when troubles set in ... So, not a marriage made in heaven, but it does have energy, and there is a chance it can work if you exercise full patience and **3** can learn to respect your need for calm now and again!

Certainly, you appreciates **3**'s glamour and charisma, and together you are sure to be popular and have a wide variety of friends. You will get on with young and old, and all will be welcome at your table. Also, there is a chance of the two of you being very lucky with money – **2** knowing how to win over difficult customers with sheer tact and charm, and **3** being able to clinch the deal with wit and spontaneous actions. Another bonus is that you are not

1   9   8   7   6   5   4   3   2

unhappy to take a secondary position in **3**'s life, to be the adviser, the aid, the support, while **3** thrills and entertains, and juggles lots of interesting options in the air.

In the end, it comes down to compromise. **3** must try to be sensitive to those moments when you need to spend time just one on one, without a visiting circus. **3** also has to ask or encourage you to give things a chance – rather than judging whether something will be wrong a priori. Maybe **3** can entice you into letting go of some of your fears and vulnerabilities; and perhaps you can get **3** to stand still long enough to listen to what you have to say. **3**s so often fend off serious discussion with an appearance of humour or being disinterested; you may need to gently persuade them to evaluate things more realistically sometimes.

So you see, this is a seesaw where the tempo and good feeling may be up one day and down the next. This is not necessarily a bad thing, for it may help you to learn just how flexible and conciliatory you can be. And **3** may

2	3	4	5	6	7	8	9	1

learn that there are some issues in life worth taking seriously: 3s aren't stupid, and have a quick, acute mind – if they would only apply it! It will be a challenge to make this partnership work ... but not an impossibility. Patience will be the key – a key that 2 holds more than the 3.

If you have another number in common, the more positive aspects of the relationship will be able to emerge, and this will make a big difference. Equally, if you have several 'C's or 'L's in your name, this will give you more tolerance of 3's nervous energy. And, of course, the sensuality you share will be a huge plus.

Key themes

Smouldering mutual attraction thanks to different but complementary styles • Very good friendship with many people • Financial and social luck together • Love affair of highs and (very often!) lows

1   9   8   7   6   5   4   3   2

2 in love with a 4 ★★★★★

In this five-star relationship, **4** understands just how important it is for **2** to have someone to listen to them. **4** is your willing audience, and respects your gentle but wise head on a vast number of subjects. **4** has the kind of attention to detail that you admire, and as lovers you have a willingness to be close and confidential with one another, which builds harmony over time. **4** isn't going to swing from chandeliers or host wild parties, but you have a mutual respect for people and moral fellow-feeling which makes you attract the friends and business partners you need to make a solid and peaceful relationship together. Moreover, **4** really loves you: it is a sincere attraction of spirit for spirit, and you have the power to influence your rock-solid **4** to become more affectionate and less utilitarian about life. **2** injects beauty and emotion into **4**'s carefully laid out garden.

2	3	4	5	6	7	8	9	1

Although there is very little friction between you, stubbornness may be the one thorn in the rose bed. **4** stands its ground like no other number, and if you feel strongly about what is at stake, there may be trouble ahead. But this is a minor point, for really **2** and **4** bring out the very best in each other. **4** not only indulges your dreams, but helps to make them into realities; and you dream such beautiful dreams, to a **4**'s taste. **4**s are not uncreative, but are often undeveloped artistically because of the need to have lived a very practical and dutiful life. **2** ends all this for **4**, and encourages their abilities in other areas. **4**s love to place their energies into their home and family, and you will never complain about this preference.

So good is the understanding between these numbers that it would suit a relationship that spills into the workplace — or you may both work in a related field. You will know when your overworking **4** needs to stop and clear their head; and your **4** will always appreciate your insights.

1   9   8   7   6   5   4   3   2

4 will also rely upon – rather than fight – your intuition, because, although such a common-sense number, 4 recognizes that not every observation is born of obvious behaviour or openness. Your ability to see what is in the dark, or around the corner, will be taken very seriously.

4 knows when you're in need of a change of scene, sensing – from personal experience – the moment when it all becomes too much. Both 2s and 4s are easily capable of working and worrying themselves into a frenzy, but no one knows the signs better than you two. And, while 4 may not be hugely imaginative about where to take you to escape for a while, you will at least have a reliable mate who has a good memory for where you have been happy before. 2 and 4 are very likely (budget permitting) to have a house in the country as a retreat – and to go there often.

4 takes on a very protective role with 2: you will feel secure with this lover. You also feel drawn to 4's stability and honesty – qualities you truly admire. Your 4 enjoys pre-

serving the traditions of the past, and allows you to indulge in some nostalgia together. Given a choice, your home may be peppered with antiques or period features, and, if you live in a newer home or city, you will somehow contrive a country, old-fashioned feel behind the modernity.

Your role, as the partner whose instincts always work overtime, is to prevent your hard-working **4** from overload, or from being sterile and staid to the exclusion of fun. If anyone can get **4** to relax it will be you, and together you should achieve harmony and practicality in equal measure. You are building, potentially, a happy world to share.

Key themes

Love of home and family • Solid approach to problems, allowing resolutions to be found • Shared interests and method in your lifestyle • **2** loosens **4**'s rigidity and cautious nature • Mutual admiration

| 1 | 9 | 8 | 7 | 6 | 5 | 4 | 3 | 2 |

2 in love with a 5   ★

An interesting one, this, for there are some strangely unexpected similarities between these numbers – although, in the main, they couldn't be more different. It could perhaps be described as 'make or break'. **2** will chafe against **5**'s chattering and restlessness, never seeming to head to any place or find any peace inside, while **5** despairs of **2** hiding their light under a bushel. And, where **5** is the pirate adventurer, **2** is the yoga student; as **5** takes on a clutch of racy ideas and opportunities, **2** is busy shaking its head, wondering whether anything will come of any of it.

But if you willingly take a back seat, and just try to trust **5**'s instincts (which are very much those of the gambler!), it could be an interesting ride. You could certainly stage-manage **5**'s brilliant performances in business, and socially, to make something extraordinary of them, and

2   3   4   5   6   7   8   9   1

your **5** will probably look to you to make them feel more secure and organized. **5** is brilliant – there is no doubt – but will it wear on you over time? These numbers are not natural friends; the one requiring gentleness and the other fireworks. And where **5** is so physical, **2** is so cerebral.

The similarities are not, at first, strikingly obvious, but on better acquaintance it will be clear that there is ground to build on between you. **5** and **2** are both people numbers, and there is a chance that **5** can widen your horizons while you bring a more discerning group of people into the home, with whom **5** can develop stronger ideas. **5** needs to be given projects, to ask for a direction to indulge in. **5** is not really practical, but tireless and full of energy. It's just that sometimes you want to be quiet and think!

And, to be fair, **2**s do sometimes snuff out **5**'s wonderful enthusiasm for life and zany brilliance. **5** is a number needing an audience, coming alive in situations that require daring. This is not to everyone's taste, but if you can lend **5** some strength and reassurance, it may be a relationship where miracles happen all around you both; and you may – as a team – affect the lives of many other people, with you being so sensitive and **5** articulating, in a striking way, the needs of the world around you. Give **5** a platform or a theatre in which to speak, and change the ordinary dullness that can be life every day. This is when your idealism cuts in, and you may think the world of your clever, inspiring **5**.

This partnership in love definitely works best if the **2** is very well-educated and philosophical, for then the **5**'s electric mind will be held by the breadth and dimension of **2**'s thinking. As the **2**, you can help to realize and actualize **5**'s ideas – concepts which will be songs in the wind unless a clever, reliable soul can plan a strategy to make use of them. **5** is a troubadour at times, and can be a wasted talent, and **2** is a dreamer, who may also let their best ideas evaporate. One of you has to get behind the other one and put smaller frictions aside to prioritize what is good. You can either widen each other's horizons, or tear away each other's gifts cruelly. **2** is more tactful, so, if you really care for this fascinating person, hold your tongue and try to make it a challenge to achieve the harmony you crave. It will be interesting, as I said in the beginning!

Key themes

Loving and ultra-sensitive **2** must learn to forgive much that **5** overlooks or deems unimportant · **5** desires freedom and their own time and space, but living with **2** can bring them more emotional security, order and refinement

2 in love with a 6   ★★★★

This is an excellent romance, with a very good chance of going the distance if you get through the first few months. Your two numbers have so many qualities that are akin – from a love of people, entertaining and nurturing, to an appreciation of what is beautiful and serene. 6 loves the good life at least as much as you do, and you will certainly create a relationship of shared interests. Travel appeals to you both, and among many arts and creative enjoyments you are both music lovers, and have a strong magnetic pull towards visual arts. In fact, keeping company together, this relationship could strengthen your individual artistic abilities as a result of the encouragement and appreciation you get from one another.

Neither of you is aggressive, which is a plus – although things may occasionally be too tranquil, with a chance that

2   3   4   5   6   7   8   9   1

the relationship could become predictable and complacent. One of you will need to think about the future, and, at various times, either one of you may take the lead in this. **6** is happy to let you dictate the terms, but you will probably feel everything can be a jointly reached decision, and this should work fairly well for both of you. Nor is it a surprise to find **6** and **2** together. You are drawn to your attractive **6**'s easy way with people and their skill in the kitchen, and they have a wonderful eye for the decorative elements of life, which will endorse your own wish to take care of how things look around you. Affection and tactility will also have a proper place in your love lives, for **6** is sensuous (if a fraction shy, perhaps) in just the same ways as you.

Your sense of tact and charm is a huge help to your **6** lover, who can feed off the confidence invested in both of you by friends, family and business partners. You are also likely to be very kind to each other about your families, with **6** taking real trouble to know how to please your relatives and friends – a favour you will return. Or, if your **6** doesn't have a big family (which will be a source of some pain to them), you are more than able to fill in the gaps and make a family of just two. In this, and in many other ways, you are co-operative and considerate of each other's feelings, hurts and highs. You also know how to help your **6** up the ladder work-wise, with gentle pressure and insistence. **6**s often languish without a nudge, and, although so attractive, kind and fascinating, they are often disappointingly inept at capitalizing on their talents. This is something you will off-set with gritty determination, for you understand the ways to bring the right people around a **6** to help them along.

You are both healers, helpers, teachers, intuitive thinkers who will make time for a life of kindness and service to others. And, blissfully, it is unlikely you will take advantage of each other in any selfish way. Even if the **2** is an **11**, it is a bond of destiny and higher thinking.

Clashes will happen only when one (or both) of you is

negative about relationships generally. If past experience has made either of you guarded, you may drive each other mad with impossible, idealistic demands which have little hope of materializing into a happy reality. You can both be dreamers, and if neither of you gets down to the business of life that is hard work, application and realism – or you allow yourselves to be walked on – the luminous potential of this relationship may meander into misfortune and sadness. However, with so many things in common, this is one of the happiest number-pairings you could wish for. Grab that lovely **6** and walk right into their heart for keeps ... for you can hardly do better!

Key themes

Share excellent taste and a wish to beautify their world together • Friends, relatives and children take priority • Lucky financially • Seen as a magnetic, attractive couple

| 1 | 9 | 8 | 7 | 6 | 5 | 4 | 3 | 2 |

2 in love with a 7   ★★

This relationship has a little more potential than the star rating might suggest – but is not an obvious success. What is good between you is that there is a chance of arriving at a harmonious day-to-day existence without much friction, but this can be a problem too. **2** and **7** may not make much progress in life together, and **7** is never an easy prospect for gentle **2**, who is unlikely to push hard enough for what they want. Thus, as the partnership-minded member of the love affair, you have to think that what may work best for tranquillity, at times, is solitude: **7** requires a great deal of time alone. If not given this physically, they will demand it by withdrawing around you and others, even when sharing the same room – which can be very frustrating.

And, your enigmatic **7** will almost never tell you what's on their mind. **7**s keep secrets from others out of

2   3   4   5   6   7   8   9   1

habit, and you may not like that at all. But what you will do is respect your intelligent lover's excellent mind, their exquisite but rather unusual taste, and find a kind of compulsion in believing you have a duty to drag them out of being unhappy or on their own, when there are times you should just leave well alone. Sometimes you may make the mistake of feeling that silence between you is serenity, because you want it so much; often, this quiet is a disguise for things that the **7** feels are wrong, and won't express. Read: danger zone.

You are likely to be more of an extrovert around your **7** than with many other numbers, for **7**'s moody nature forces you forwards and **7** appreciates your charm and gentleness – even seeks your seemingly calm manner with people – because it is not their way. They can be so witty, perhaps even cutting, that it makes you laugh out loud, but this way of looking a little cynically at the world is not your preferred approach. You will be cross if you think your **7**'s fine mind is being wasted on a feeling that it is all hopeless and that nothing can change.

If I am making this all sound negative, that is unfair, for there are many wonderful things that may emerge in this relationship, depending on how many negative character-istics have taken root in each of you. **7**'s positive attributes sit well with **2**'s – an interest in metaphysical or occult thinking, and a high regard for spiritual rather than material truths. Plus, if you are fairly self-confident and feel opti-mistic about the life you have brought into being around you, you may be just the person who can co-operate with your fascinating love, and allow them the time they need to meditate on what is important, and to devise a way of existing with grace in the world you find yourselves in.

This partnership works best if the female is the **2**, as **7** is truly in awe of **2**'s femininity. Equally, if **7** is forced to take a protective role with **2**, it may bring out their strengths. And it all works a lot better if the **2** is an **11**. But even then,

friendship or a mad fling might be better than an expectation of a really long-lasting bond, because **2**s will always
want more diverse company and fun than **7**s, who can be
very set in a pattern of privacy and retreat inside their mind
too often. Plus, **7** gets irritated by **2**'s frequent forays into
mothering the world! And, strangely enough, **7** can be more
practical than **2** – although no one may see it that way.

Attraction between you, then, is no surprise, but for
this to work long-term much negotiation between differing
needs and underlying world views must be achieved. If you
want to badly enough, you may find a way to do just that.

Key themes

Shared quiet time, but sometimes emotions aren't
properly expressed · Respect for each other's intelligence;
2 looks up to **7** for their excellent mind · **7** prefers few
friends of high calibre, while **2** gets on with most people

| 1 | 9 | 8 | 7 | 6 | 5 | 4 | 3 | 2 |

2 in love with an 8   ★★★★

This is one of the best partnerships in town – especially if
the **2** is an **11**. You respect **8**'s fairness to others and their
ability (not unlike your own) of seeing both sides of an
argument and caring for the underdog. You are good souls
in a world of doubters, two people who not only think they
can make a difference by being strong and kind to others,
but who are *willing to do it*. And you love **8**'s sense of control – their generosity and warmth. Yes – this relationship
has serious potential.

8 is a number made up of two circles: a higher and a
lower world. What will excite you is the way **8** can balance
a material life with a spiritual and philosophical one. And,
like you, **8** is musical (the number spells the octave, and
has natural rhythm). You may be more likely to find financial harmony with an **8** than anyone else, and lucky **8** has

2   3   4   5   6   7   8   9   1

you to help them juggle all the requirements of being a good lover, a good citizen, a good business entrepreneur and a good parent. This is a co-operative partnership.

You like **8**'s honesty combined with tact, which gains even more emphasis from teamwork with you, and their appreciation of fine objects, and you are willing to build a beautiful home and chic life around them. This is also a very physical bond – one of the best number-partnerships for you to enjoy a strongly sensual as well as practical dimension: friends as well as lovers, let's say. **8**'s humour, style and flamboyance are a foil to your subtlety and finesse. When you combine your energies, you tow each other along into more pleasure, more experience. **2** reminds **8**, crucially, of the need to stop sometimes and just play, or talk, or rest – and **8** is willing to be reminded.

As a couple, you are quite likely to be spiritual (just as with a **7**), but an **8** lover also invites you to join in with the highbrow world of successful people, and you will be in

1   9   8   7   6   5   4   3   2

your element here. And, it must be said, you add as much to **8**'s brilliant world as anyone can. You are a delicate business ally, a good listener when **8** has to talk out loud to think, and you offer very good advice, which **8** willingly heeds. This works both ways, and sometimes you will feel your **8** is voicing the very things you were thinking, so well-tuned are your minds.

What works between you works very well. The only thing you may have to guard against is a propensity to think a little too well of your **8**, who is, after all, only mortal, and will make mistakes. **8**s see so many options and opportunities, but are sometimes spendthrift and too generous, which you can help to counterbalance with good sense. For some reason, **8** and **2** like to live up high together — whether in a tall block or penthouse, or in a home with a view. Perhaps this is because their lofty thinking really takes flight when they are in the clouds.

Together, **8** and **2** exude a kind of nobility, and offer friends a safe haven in times of stress. **8** often adds professional thought or knowledge to **2**'s exceptional insights, and you will gain a reputation with others for being efficient and fair. **2** reminds **8** of important causes that need help; **8** reminds **2** to be optimistic when the chips are down. Alternately serene together and people-loving, your moods should blend rather than annoy each other, and you will, if anything, enhance each other's individual wisdom with shared observation and conversation. A truly positive opportunity for a happy relationship that should be able to redress momentary lapses of individualism.

Key themes

2 has calming effect on **8** • **8** understands and values **2**'s contributions emotionally and intellectually • Music and material enjoyment important to both, though you are generous to others too

| 1 | 9 | 8 | 7 | 6 | 5 | 4 | 3 | 2 |

2 in love with a 9   ★★★

Though only scoring three stars, this relationship may do very well. **2s** have a basic instinct with partnerships of all kinds, and **9s** are loving souls in a 'cuddle-the-world' sort of way. You will be very impressed by the breadth of **9**'s thinking, and **9s** have a way of making **2s** feel better about themselves, thanks to their good habit of listening to what you have to say – even encouraging you to talk. This is especially true if you are an **11: 9** feels for you, and you may be the one person who can prod them out of the abstract-thinking phase and into action.

Storms arise when **9** goes negative, which happens not infrequently, for your sensitive **9** is a mirror of other people's feelings. This is hard on you, because you're not aggressive and will be more inclined to suffer alongside your beloved than issue ultimatums. **9s** also carry some

2   3   4   5   6   7   8   9   1

serious emotional baggage from the past — concerning parents and past lovers — and may not always be able to extricate themselves from tangles. In fact, **9** somehow manages to get caught up in emotionally complicated relationships and draws compliant **2** in, as well — which may be fine if you can play the no-nonsense counsellor, but this is rarely the case with **2** when love is in the air!

But what works well works very well. You broaden each other's horizons, and have a willingness to learn from one another; and **9** may goad you gently into disciplining your own good mind more than anyone else can. Add to this a pinch of seascape — because you are drawn to, and flourish by, the sea together — and an interest shared in words, and many good things could be borne of this relationship. Your **9** needs a true companion, and you may offer this, but you will need to allow your **9** some personal freedoms to go off alone, or with friends, for if you are too cloying, and demonstrate any insecurity, **9** will be frustrated and angry and lose their exceptional goodwill.

The way to make this relationship work is to take each other by the hand and find a cause to share – whether that is study, family, politics, or your children's education. When far-seeing **9** borrows **2**'s tact and diplomatic skill, anything can happen. And the personal relationship will prosper as long as you, **2**, don't need constant reassurances that you're loved or being considered, for this will bore **9**. If you keep your sense of mystery, so that **9** is always wondering what makes you tick, you will have a very good chance of keeping one another enthralled.

On the positive side, you will be attracted to a life of variety, as **9** excites you to be more adventurous than usual. Some **2**s remain a homebody, but **9** will never settle for this, and needs fresh stimulation. This gives you more scope and allows you, as a pair, to grow. Part of what you find so deeply magnetic about your **9** is their call to know more about the world, so you will have to go along

| 2 | 3 | 4 | 5 | 6 | 7 | 8 | 9 | 1 |

with this and resign some quietness for the party lifestyle. It will be worth it.

One piece of advice: don't aggravate **9** about the past. Like **7**s, **9**s bottle up some emotions and reactions. Over time, if anyone can gain their trust and get them to open up it will be you, but don't force these issues unless you are trying to create dramas. The relationship may not take the strain. Gentleness and patience are required somewhere along the line, so be willing to let this bond find its own pace, and go with it rather than trying to remould or redirect it. If you can do this, many good things may unfold.

Key themes

9 will probably take the lead, but **2** assists and helps them finish what they start • Good understanding of people • Shared taste, to a degree — especially for literature, film and art • **9** needs emotional privacy about the past!

| 1 | 9 | 8 | 7 | 6 | 5 | 4 | 3 | 2 |

2 in love with an 11 ★★★★

This can be extremely exciting. Here is a relationship between two essentially like-minded souls, but with the number 11 thrown into the equation there is a natural leader and a steady anchor. Heaven knows 11s are glamorous and interesting – never settling for the same routine life as other people – but they can be so flighty and unstable, so given to extremes, so emotionally unpredictable. The blessing here is that the pure 2 has the lack of ego and kind heart, as well as that crucial intuition which tells them how 11 is feeling, to create an even keel for 11. This pairing has more buzz and sexual electricity than two 2s, but also an element of surprise about it which could be 'make or break'.

What an 11 does in partnership with a 2 is pure poetry. Sure, there is an automatic tendency to take the

2 3 4 5 6 7 8 9 1

lead and feel protective to **2**, because the dynamism of the 'double **1**' can't help forging ahead and making things happen in life. **2**, of course, has the largesse of spirit and the instinctive understanding to see this as desirable – and selflessly sings **11**'s praises, bringing the security for **11** to do clever things and be an amazing, vibrant and romantic lover.

But let us not underestimate what **2** adds for an **11**. Not everyone understands **11**'s mindset, as they sometimes seem to be living in a world of their own. Emotionally, **11**s are more intense than **2**s, wanting to find unusual ways of expressing and exploring relationships. But they are also subject to rejection and, because **11** is always made up of two digits, it is as though they never have both feet on the floor at the same time. In love affairs this can be very heartbreaking for **11**, who feels they give all and have such a huge heart (all true!), which nevertheless confuses the object of their affection. This is where **2**'s inner calm and wonderful powers of perception come to the rescue. **2** is magnetically pulled to **11**, recognizing a kindred soul with a zest for life, and the enormous physical and mental stamina to bring dreams to fruition. **2**'s role as anchor is vital to **11**'s success.

And so the love between these numbers can soar to its height. Both of you love beautiful things and are excellent hosts, and you each have an appreciation and respect for the other's individuality; together you have a warmth and vitality which permeates the world around you. Romantic, sexy, artistic and relatively secure materially (although **11**s do oscillate from rags to riches at times!), this partnership should be set for fun, love and longevity if it survives the getting-to-know-you phase. **2** won't get a medal for putting up with **11**'s over-sensitive tantrums early on, but if they see past them they are on the road to a great bond for life. As with all **2** relationships — and this is no exception — co-operation is the key.

| 2 | 3 | 4 | 5 | 6 | 7 | 8 | 9 | 1 |

Potential strife comes from the similarity between you, and the fact that you recognize so many traits – both attractive and unattractive – in one another. You bring out the best, but also the worst, in each other. You both want to lead, and are both used to attracting attention and admiration from your followers. If you can agree on which way you want to go, you will build a heaven; but if you antagonize and disorientate one another, you're building more of a hell. This is a perfect match or a perfect mismatch, and which it is will depend on how you organize your exceptional combined talents and visions.

Key themes

Life goes up a gear • Romance and passion on the menu • Arguments will occur, but **2** is patient of **11**'s tantrums • Well suited in most areas, once the courtship settles into love

| 1 | 9 | 8 | 7 | 6 | 5 | 4 | 3 | 2 |

2 in love with a 22   ★★★★★

As with **11**, this soul attracts you strongly. You are even better designed for each other than **2** and **11**, because you recognize that **22**s are very special. Organized and confident, yet calm, in love **22** may be excitable but unruffled with you. **22** is patient of **2**'s dreams, and you will love their outlook, their taste, the way they enter a room with quiet authority, their awareness – without ego – that they have a slight superiority to nearly everyone around them. This hooks you, for you love an intelligent, capable, serene soul who looks as though nothing can derail their career intentions and the things they hold important. This is someone you want to know very well – a lover you want to get behind and help. You will happily espouse their causes and be the most able of assistants – nor will all-seeing **22** omit to thank you for your considerable contributions.

| 2 | 3 | 4 | 5 | 6 | 7 | 8 | 9 | 1 |

Your **22** will not be pushed around, emotionally speaking, and you will have to fit in. This will be more difficult if you're an **11**, for then there is a chance of two great, out-of-the-ordinary minds locking horns and going into combat. Essentially you both have different ways of seeing what will make a fulfilling, intellectually challenging life, and are more than willing to suffer without personal comforts for the sake of a bigger picture. But occasionally that contrast in the way you feel goals should be achieved causes the temperature to rise. Better if this is a **22** and a pure **2**, who will settle into a natural, affectionate working order.

And no one brings out **2**'s romance and capacity for passion more than charismatic **22**. Feeling secure and proud of someone who is, at base, essentially a practical and intelligent **4**, you feel the freedom to fly a little, to let go of personal doubts and anxieties and feel truly loved. This makes a creative lover – someone who is willing to try anything once – and a **22** will lead you to find your highest powers of expression and thinking. **22** is a drifter, travels as part of the daily requirement of life, probably having left behind one secure but limiting lifestyle to move into something more challenging. All of this excites **2** (and **11**), and makes you an excellent double act, with your sense and everyday courage helping **22** out of those tight corners that accompany a life different from the crowd. **22** can be restless, but you know how to help them unwind. And lest I make **22** sound too Olympian, they can be stubborn and intractable – which is when you can manipulate them gently into a more pragmatic stance.

Whether you're **2** or **11**, you should be able to help your **22** find some equilibrium, for **22** lives off quite a bit of nervous energy (unlike a **4**), and likes to work through any project until it's realized. This can mean long hours, travel commitments, late nights. Someone in love with such a person must be tolerant of this demanding lifestyle, and **2** can be this someone. You may even prevent the overwork that is such a potential emotional stress for **22**, and the one thing that can cost them a relationship.

If you're prepared to get involved with one of life's achievers, this may be the best love affair in the world for you. This is not to say there won't be highs and lows, or lonely times; nor does it promise that **22**'s stubbornness won't sometimes cause more than a wrinkle in your eyebrow. It comes down to what is important – and **2** can almost always share **22**'s vision. As a reward, life will never be humdrum, love will never be mild. **22** cares to make you happy, and cares that you care. Potentially, your best love.

Key themes

Create happiness together • Understand each other's strengths and versatility • **22** gains respect for **2**'s contributions • **2** intuits what **22** is worrying about and remedies it

1   9   8   7   6   5   4   3   2

Work

YOUR **WORK** COMPATIBILITY CHART

	1	2	3	4	5
With a 1	★★★★	★★★★★	★	★★★	★★★
With a 2	★★★★★	★★★	★★★	★★★★	★
With a 3	★	★★★	★★★★	★★	★★★★★
With a 4	★★★	★★★★	★★	★★★★★	★★★
With a 5	★★★	★	★★★★★	★★★	★★
With a 6	★★	★★★★★	★★★★	★★★★	★★★★
With a 7	★★★★★	★★★	★★★	★★★★★	★★
With an 8	★★★★★	★★★★★	★★★★★	★★★	★★★★
With a 9	★★★★	★★★	★★★★★	★★	★★★
With an 11	★★	★★★★	★★★	★★★★★	★★
With a 22	★★★★★	★★	★★★	★★★	★★★★

2   3   4   5   6   7   8   9   1

6	7	8	9	11	22
★★	★★★★★	★★★★★	★★★★	★★	★★★★★
★★★★★	★★★	★★★★★	★★★	★★★★	★★
★★★★	★★★	★★★★★	★★★★★	★★★	★★★
★★★★	★★★★★	★★★	★★	★★★★★	★★★
★★★★	★★	★★★★	★★★	★★	★★★★
★★★	★	★★★★	★★★	★★★★★	★★★★
★	★★★★	★★★	★★	★★★★	★★★★★
★★★★	★★★	★★★	★★★★	★★★★★	★★★★
★★★	★★	★★★★	★★★	★★★★★	★★★★★
★★★★★	★★★★	★★★★★	★★★★★	★★★★	★★★★★
★★★★	★★★★★	★★★★	★★★★★	★★★★★	★★★

| 1 | 9 | 8 | 7 | 6 | 5 | 4 | 3 | 2 |

2 working with a 1   ★★★★★

This is the co-worker you've been longing for. Diplomatic **2** understands just what is required before **1** has asked, bringing you tea or organizing lunch: this is a five-star working relationship. This assessment *does* work on the assumption that **1** is giving the orders, though. If the **2** tries to tell **1** what to do, big ego adjustments may be required — and, in fact, you would rather be the quieter partner anyway. But the energy you manage to generate together is highly effective, and there will also be a feeling of harmony in the environment you work in together. In short, **2** keeps high-voltage **1** calm.

Occasionally, **1** feels you may be a doormat, or forgets to say 'thank you' when you fill your usual role of seeing to their needs. This word is easy to omit, because you never ask for it, and **1** may seem oblivious; but by never saying it

1 is ruining a good relationship. A **2** at work is gentle and efficient but not weak, so remind **1** of their manners!

2 always looks on **1**'s creativity with appreciation, and admires their ambition and focus; you often also ignore **1**'s aggressive streak, as you nobly understand that it can be positive, and have a desirable outcome. **1** must not say unkind things, though, or tease you, for you have a bursting point. You function smoothly at work, support everyone, get on with most people, but you don't give in on the odd occasion you reach your own conclusion – even if it differs from bossy **1**'s. Just sometimes, **1** must give in gracefully. **1** trusts your intuition with others at work, and if you dig your heels in will understand you have good reason.

Key themes

Smooth running · Calm space · Efficient · Good understanding

| 1 | 9 | 8 | 7 | 6 | 5 | 4 | 3 | 2 |

2 working with a 2 ★★★

2 and **2** makes **4**, an enviable team. Of course, you need to assign different spheres for expression, so that you each have domain over what interests you best. However, the usual outcome of two **2**s in business is of a gently structured partnership where each one is willing to do whatever it takes to make things work well and harmoniously, both for themselves and others. With another **2** you can be honest, and you will always know exactly where you are. You understand each other's instincts brilliantly.

If there are other people in your business lives, they will appreciate the way you work together, filling in words for others before they have spoken them, perceptively recognizing when there is a problem causing others stress or unhappiness. Like a crew on a yacht in high seas, you are rarely thrown by problems or emergencies, and you are, as ever, selfless enough to work in sync without expectation of applause – and you earn respect from everyone around you.

This is why two **2**s working together are likely to have formed some kind of partnership of their own, rather than working for others. Or, if you do work for a larger company, chances are your own area will seem serenely autonomous. You function well and are considerate of others, and you lift each other's creative instincts because you read one another so well. Confidence inspires productivity, and you will achieve tremendous goals, which others will find baffling, given they see you both as so relatively mild. But be careful of overwork, as two of you together may forget when to call it a day – or to demand time off when you need it!

Key themes

Instinctive · Respectful · Good bonhomie with colleagues · Efficient team work

| 1 | 9 | 8 | 7 | 6 | 5 | 4 | 3 | 2 |

2 working with a 3   ★★★

You like **3**'s creativity but are driven mad by their lack of organization. Both of you find it hard to push for a clear decision, and you will be irritated when **3** introduces yet another set of options. **3** does things so differently from you, and you have doubts about their concentration and commitment, but there are positives. **3** recognizes **2**'s ability to work behind the scenes with difficult customers, and, as **3** is such a good upfront person, this could be workable if you are given different arenas to move about in.

3 seems too flash for **2**, who prefers to be quiet and subtle, while **2** feels too cautious for **3**, who always likes to take chances in business – and usually pulls them off. **2** will be annoyed by **3**'s manner of chatting and being informal with everyone, and **3** will be frustrated when **2** pours water on their unusual but brilliant ideas. But, given

| 2 | 3 | 4 | 5 | 6 | 7 | 8 | 9 | 1 |

that **2** is so willing to be amicable, this work team can achieve a great deal if you just agree to do things differently and get on with it. **3** appreciates **2**'s negotiation skills, and values their more demure style of aesthetic input. **3** has the pizzazz, but **2** the taste – and, married, this can be an interesting cross-pollination.

Some days, **3** will amuse you and make you laugh just when you need it – when deadlines are too close, or personal pressures are at a peak. This is what **3** *can* do for you. And you can slow **3**'s racing pulse when they get a little too excitable. Just remember to accept that this is a swing, up one day, down the next, and to be your most tolerant self when things get too noisy!

Key themes

Creative • Good with people • Indecisive • Different working techniques

| 1 | 9 | 8 | 7 | 6 | 5 | 4 | 3 | 2 |

2 working with a 4 ★★★★

Two people who always get on well, this can be a very constructive relationship in the office. **2** appreciates the strength of **4**'s method and approach to getting the job done, while **4** has a clear understanding of what it takes to translate ideas into reality, relying on **2**'s excellent judgement with people and willingness to do what's required for the good of the whole. **4** sees you as the specialist people-motivator you are; less observant numbers miss this.

4s are passionate about a job well done. Not a number to tap-dance in the moonlight without extreme provocation, **4** can take genuine delight in doing something difficult with precision, and you admire this tenacity and skill. Where **4** can be blunt, or forget to speak at all when wrapped up in a project, you assuage feelings of neglect, or fill in missing details for others. The one seems to take over

2   3   4   5   6   7   8   9   1

exactly where the other leaves off. Add to this the way you inspire **4** to get the point and are then happy to take a pew beside them through thick and thin, and anyone can see why these numbers are good for each other.

There are very small dangers in a **2/4** business relationship, which mainly relate to self-deprecation and overwork, respectively. **4** would like to see you get more of the praise you richly deserve, but, being a **2**, you will almost never ask for it. However, rest assured you have an ally and reliable friend who will never turn against you. **4** will need you to be supportive too, because this is not a number that sells itself to other more flamboyant members of a working group. **4** is misunderstood by many, but never by **2**.

Key themes
Complementary abilities · **2** a people person and **4** a slogger who delivers the impossible without fireworks

| 1 | 9 | 8 | 7 | 6 | 5 | 4 | 3 | 2 |

2 working with a 5 ★

This is a tricky work relationship, because **2** doesn't understand what makes **5** tick in business — and that is unusual.
2s have such a hold on most people's inner motives, hearing words unspoken; and perhaps therein lies the difficulty.
5 is almost never silent — always talking things up and
achieving much that is extraordinary through pure chat.
You believe this is the sign of a phoney, and don't trust **5**,
appreciating inner stillness and focus rather than **5**'s
method of making a splash with the perfect bon mot. By
5's standards, **2** is old-fashioned or over-cautious and, as
in romance, it is not always easy to smooth the ruffled
feathers of a **5** and a **2** working in nearly any context.

   Perhaps the best chance for harmony is if the **5** starts
out in a junior capacity and has to rely on their considerable charm to win the **2** over from the first. This may lead

| 2 | 3 | 4 | 5 | 6 | 7 | 8 | 9 | 1 |

to a lasting truce, and a grudging willingness on the **2**'s part to admire a personality at work whose talents can be measured in results. **2**, then, may be quietly amused and accepting, but will hardly be converted to cheeky **5**'s advertising-executive way. **2** would always rather do things with control, and the solid attributes of the **4** that are so suited to a **2**'s working make-up are exactly what is missing in the gambling, inspirational **5**, who is never bland enough to appeal to everyone. This is a shame, given that **5** might flourish with **2**'s careful hands taking the wheel.

The best approach for these two numbers is to give them a great divide and let them deal with it as best they can. At least it will entertain everyone around them!

Key themes

Underlying tension • Two very different personalities with little overlap of method

| 1 | 9 | 8 | 7 | 6 | 5 | 4 | 3 | 2 |

2 working with a 6   ★★★★★

Because of a productive understanding that exists between your two numbers, **6** and **2** are very well suited to working in business. **6** has such a delicate understanding of what **2** is doing, even without being told, that a subtle shift of direction in a meeting is instantly understood by the **6**. And **2** – always able to compute in an instant where the ground has shifted to – relies on the equally conciliatory **6** to get unwilling customers to agree to just about anything. No other numbers handle other individuals better, or have more aesthetic appreciation for making an uplifting environment seem the most desirable place to be. Any work space that houses a **6** and **2** working together will exude a calm beauty where everyone is happy to be.

Add to this the fact that both numbers are creative and like the beautiful things in life – being thus prepared to work steadily for them – and we have a recipe for financial success. Interestingly, there is, perhaps, no natural leader here. **6** will be as willing to work as your assistant as you would be to work as theirs; this may culminate in a work situation which sees no bosses, but several happy partners!

When you add both numbers together, we come to **8**: the number of money. Nothing else spells out so well how much potential these numbers have together, should they go into a business partnership. Though seemingly quiet and not at all attention-grabbing, **2** and **6** will seize the day without being noticed. If the business has anything to do with the beauty industry, music, the arts or teaching/healing, it will be highly successful and happy. A five-star team.

Key themes
Achieve a serene and aesthetically uplifting environment together • Please everyone they deal with

| 1 | 9 | 8 | 7 | 6 | 5 | 4 | 3 | 2 |

2 working with a 7   ★★★

This relationship works very well in specialist areas, as this brings out the best in **7**, and **2** will be a detailed and organized helpmate. **7** loves to hone its mind on what is difficult to perfect – taking up challenges no one else wants to touch. **2** is a wonderful support here, because both numbers succeed well in research areas, and don't need a party atmosphere to feel work is rewarding. Your goals are similar, and you share a love of a job really well done. Plus, **2** has great admiration for **7**'s intelligence and inner stillness.

More than this, **2** can deflect public attention or distractions away from **7** when it has its head down. **7**'s challenge is just to get on with the job and produce something as perfect as possible, without having to explain intentions to outside parties. **2** realizes this, and wants to protect high-minded **7** from irritations that slow up the process.

2	3	4	5	6	7	8	9	1

Things can go sour if **7** is arrogant – which sometimes happens! – so that you feel patronized or overlooked. You always have contributions to make that are worth hearing; but sometimes **7** becomes so fixated on their own plans that there is little consultation with others, and you become aggrieved by this neglect. The other problem is that **7**s often take their personal woes out on others without meaning to – but there's never an explanation or apology. As an intuitive **2** you realize this is the case, but feel indignation that they are unable to be honest about this simple thing with others – to the potential detriment of group harmony. Overall, though, the energy between **2** and **7** in the workplace is good and produces excellent results.

Key themes

Innate understanding · Mutual respect · Attention to detail · Research work ideal

1 9 8 7 6 5 4 3 2

2 working with an 8　★★★★★

An excellent inner communication and effortless feeling of harmony that affects all is produced here. You share the same instincts for what works, what pleases, and how to get others on board. There is, simply, a rapport between you.

There is always a feeling of expectation around **2** and **8**. Perhaps there is a frisson of attraction which sets up the added dynamic; or, it could be the way one understands the other without redundant explanation. It is so good that it would make an excellent business partnership where you each work for yourselves. **8** will have the dream of higher remuneration, and you back this up with earthy suggestions **8** respects. You humour **8** when necessary, and make a lighter atmosphere, which is good for everyday tranquillity. Best of all, you pre-empt **8**'s needs, and know before they do what will be required in a project that may only be in its planning phase, astonishing them by producing facts at the appropriate moment like so many rabbits from hats.

Even when emergencies arise – which they will, as you push **8**'s ability to the wire – you have a knack together of resolving any crisis before it becomes too threatening. This is partly because **2** diffuses the tension, and helps **8** maintain the steely control and determination for which they are justly famous. And, if **8** seems to be the dynamo, don't imagine **2**'s vital role as anchor, bantering charmer and organized thinker is overlooked – least of all by the **8**, who will sing your praises even when you have no way of knowing. This is potentially a truly excellent work relationship waiting to take off and make something new and fun.

Key themes

Inspire each other's strengths • Work with humour and instinct • Balance each other's needs • Frisson of attraction?

| 1 | 9 | 8 | 7 | 6 | 5 | 4 | 3 | 2 |

2 working with a 9　　★★★

Together, these two are rowing in the same direction. **9** assumes a patriarchal protectiveness of **2**, but with good intentions, and **2** understands this, refusing to take offence. As a sensitive **2**, you gently assuage **9**'s doubts about what is possible, pushing them to strive for the best (which is considerable, from a **9**). Often it is only disorganization that prevents **9** from flying high, and **2** easily offsets this by taking care of details and filling in behind **9**, who can be a showman, while keeping everyone calm and happy. You often help **9** finish projects others have set in motion, and both of you create an atmosphere of ease for the people who work around you. **9** keeps you feeling upbeat, and you prevent **9** from worrying about what may never happen. Countering **9**'s potential for negativity is a great **2** skill.

You sense which of **9**'s dreams can become realities

2　　3　　4　　5　　6　　7　　8　　9　　1

and which are pie in the sky, and quietly promote to others what **9** has to offer. As repayment, **9** is the number who can best verbalize your feelings of what may be contributed; you are never your own best press agent. **9** gets on with almost everyone, and their approach to life can expand your social conscience. Work-wise, you will find the most productive way of tackling problems from sheer willingness to do so.

9 will sometimes annoy you, mainly when you feel situations could be handled more efficiently. You may also feel cross that they want to be too many things to too many people, failing to concentrate on what they could do so well. But if anyone can smooth out these difficulties and show **9** where to put its energies, that person is **2**.

Key themes

Complementary talents • **9**'s moodiness confuses **2** • **2** gets on board with **9**'s plans

1	9	8	7	6	5	4	3	2

2 working with an 11   ★★★★

This goes up a notch from two **2**s. **2** has the patience to understand what is in the **11**'s head, recognizing brilliance and a need for harnessing and channelling the **11**'s energy and ideas. **11** is very creative, and has more ego and fire than **2**; but, without being wrong-footed by this, **2** simply sees what must be done to make the **11**'s ideas manageable. The **11** is likely to be in a frontline position, but the **2** is better organized than the **11**, not having the two digits to negotiate. These two digits make for a permanent sense of electricity but also a dip and rise in moods, optimism, strength. **2** makes the difference and evens out the score.

If we accept that there is little need for competition between you, you have the grit to work tirelessly together for extended periods. Perhaps the **11** will occasionally frustrate the **2**, by becoming irritable with others who can't understand what they have said at first go. **2** shrugs, amused but unable to help: **11** just has to slow down and *explain* sometimes. And **11** is high-handed with mortals, wondering where is their spirit, vision, imagination. **11** also becomes outraged at any lack of justice, where **2** is more resigned to realism – if no less disappointed. But **2** working with **11** irons out some of this smouldering, volcanic energy. In a business partnership of any sort, these numbers work very well – as long as **11** feels it is given some free rein!

The best opportunities for doing well together are in creative or artistic fields, or the media – or anything that demands a relationship with the public. You have a good feel for what appeals to public taste!

Key themes

Mutual understanding · Good blend of the possible with the impossible · Excellent for work in a public arena

| 1 | 9 | 8 | 7 | 6 | 5 | 4 | 3 | 2 |

2 working with a 22 ★★

This works less well than one feels it should on paper – and certainly not nearly as well as it does when the relationship is personal and emotional. In business, **22** becomes steely and professional, not always happy to break from what it is fixated on, and very often forgetting to explain/talk/liaise/consult with anyone else. **22** thinks everyone understands this, and that it's OK, and **2** feels a bristling annoyance that **22** can be so, well, selfish!

You won't be put off by **22**'s insistence of assuming responsibility over others: this seems right, and a **2** never begrudges a leader who does a job well. What does stop you in your tracks is that a **22** on the path to its own destiny takes everything to a higher plateau – looking for work fulfilment with people in positions of power, or becoming an impersonal, global thinker. This, you feel, ignores the little person. And sometimes, perhaps, that's true.

22 creates a world on the material plane – actual physicalities and infrastructures – while **2** cares for humanities and people. This may create a collision course, because questions of ethics and morals come into the work a **22** does every day, and you may feel that certain small details get lost in this equation. **22** doesn't forget about individuals as much as you may think, but there is definitely a difference of opinion between you as to what is important, what is enduring, and what is justifiable. So, while **2** can definitely lend **22** method and take on a great deal of their minutiae, **22** may lose **2**'s complete confidence over time.

Key themes

Differing opinions of what is important in life · **2** recognizes **22**'s amazing skills, but may find them impersonal and lacking perspective

1   9   8   7   6   5   4   3   2

Friendship

YOUR **FRIENDSHIP** COMPATIBILITY CHART

	1	2	3	4	5
With a 1	★★★	★★★★★	★★	★★★	★★★
With a 2	★★★★★	★★	★★★	★★★★	★
With a 3	★★	★★★	★★★★	★	★★★★
With a 4	★★★	★★★★	★	★★★★★	★★
With a 5	★★★	★	★★★★	★★	★★★
With a 6	★	★★★★	★★★★★	★★★	★★★★
With a 7	★★★★	★★★★★	★★★★	★★★★★	★
With an 8	★★★★	★★★★	★★★★★	★★	★★★★
With a 9	★★★★	★★★	★★★★	★★★★	★★★★
With an 11	★★★	★★★★★	★★	★★★★★	★★
With a 22	★★★	★★★	★★★★	★★	★★★

| 2 | 3 | 4 | 5 | 6 | 7 | 8 | 9 | 1 |

6	7	8	9	11	22
★	★★★★	★★★★	★★★★	★★★	★★★
★★★★	★★★★★	★★★★	★★★	★★★★★	★★★
★★★★★	★★★★	★★★★★	★★★★	★★	★★★★
★★★	★★★★★	★★	★★★★	★★★★★	★★
★★★★	★	★★★★	★★★★	★★	★★★
★★★★	★	★★★★	★★★★	★★★	★★★★★
★	★★★★	★★★	★★	★★★★★	★★★★★
★★★★	★★★	★★★★	★★★★	★★★★★	★★★
★★★★	★★	★★★★	★★	★★★★	★★★★
★★★	★★★★★	★★★★★	★★★★	★★★★★	★★★★
★★★★★	★★★★★	★★★	★★★★	★★★★	★★

1	9	8	7	6	5	4	3	2

You get on well with nearly everyone, though you sometimes feel others may have their priorities in the wrong place. Let's see which are the best combinations ... and which are the worst:

2 and 1 (★★★★★): As with all other relationships, there is a natural pecking order which sees **1** take the leading role, with **2** mostly happy in a supporting part. **1**s know that their **2** friends quietly tell them the truth, and know how to mollify their moods!

2 and 2 (★★): You have too much, perhaps, in common, and friendship can be strained. You know one another's weak spots a little too well and may hit out at them — though mutual understanding of each other's pain and sensitivity does offer some common ground.

2 and 3 (★★★): You are people-loving and sociable, but **3**'s methods are a little too scatty for you! **3** has so many balls in the air that it will bring a censorious reaction from you. Also, you think **3** fickle about their love interests. Good pals, but not too close.

2 and 4 (★★★★): These people make good friends to many numbers, but you will find them truly reliable and loyal. **4**s interest you because you know there is more to them: they don't give all their feelings utterance, but you guess – and understand!

2 and 5 (★): Different styles about everything here. **5** seems short-sighted to you, under-valuing things you feel have great merit. They may be too blasé, or not care deeply about people you think are more deserving – but then **5** may think you too serious and strait-laced, as well!

1   9   8   7   6   5   4   3   2

2 and **6** (★★★★): You will probably keep all the **6** friends you make. Your values and interests are aligned, and you understand things in the same way. **6** values your sensitivity and warmth, and you appreciate their feelings for others. You will bring each other through some tender times.

2 and **7** (★★★★★): Kindred spirits, to a huge degree. Those things that would irritate you about **7** in a romance are an inspiration to you in friendship – **7** takes on the world and never backs off if there's a moral point in the argument. You get on board, and add considerable charm and weight.

2 and **8** (★★★★): Take the elements that work well between you in love, and these same truths dictate good friendship. **8** relies on your good judgement – which so often corroborates theirs. You think, feel, believe in similar things, and your ability to see both sides of an argument works for each of you. Lifelong chums.

| 2 | 3 | 4 | 5 | 6 | 7 | 8 | 9 | 1 |

2 and **9** (★★★): Another strong friendship. All the higher numbers understand your true strength and don't mistake gentleness for weakness. You bring an ingredient of practical thinking and management to the **9**, who is often a shade lofty, and **9** bolsters your self-belief.

2 and **11** (★★★★★): Though pure **2**s often grate against each other, this is converted to a really powerful tie when one of you is a master number. **11** does take the higher hand, perhaps, but the **2** adds sense and necessary inner calm, which helps **11** take flight in every sense.

2 and **22** (★★★): A friend you sincerely admire and want to support. **22** may confuse you more than **11**, only because they seem more impersonal and not as gritty about life. Still, you enjoy **22** 's quiet humour and good mind, and you lead each other to areas of interest you would not have found independently.

1   9   8   7   6   5   4   3   2

2 IN OTHER PLACES

So what does it mean when your number turns up on a house? Do you live in a 2 home? And how does the number 2 affect your pet – or even the car that you drive? Numbers exude a subtle influence on everything in our lives; and here are just a few examples of how ...

2   3   4   5   6   7   8   9   1

A 2 address

If the number of your address — or of your apartment — reduces back to a **2**, it will be a haven for a couple! This address is ideal for a love nest just for two to share, and it will be both peaceful and uplifting to the spirit. Music will spill forth from the windows in gentle harmony, and this home should be decorated in tasteful colours with a hint of pink-gold to bring its serenity and beauty to the fore.

As soon as a third person looms to invade a **2** house, it may seem crowded. Certainly, even when it is a large enough dwelling, there is something perfect about a **2** house for two owners. But if it does survive a larger family taking it on, it will always preserve an aspect of the tranquil cottage that is romantic and neatly proportioned. Don't be surprised if a **2** house sees a business partnership run from somewhere within its four walls — at least part-time. It suits the home's character!

A 2 pet

If you don't know your pet's birthday, use the first letter of their name to calculate their number. If it's a B, K or T, they're a **2**. This is an affectionate pet, who is happy to be with you. When you sit, it snuggles beside you (not helpful, if it's rather large!), and it also likes more than one person to be close to. Sensitive and intuitive, this **2** cat knows what you will say before you say it, or **2** dog understands when something is wrong or someone's unhappy. And, if you're tired or cranky, this animal had better run for cover, needing a peaceful environment in which to prosper.

Your **2** pet has wonderful taste. How can you be sure of this? Well, it will seek the most tactile and graceful chair, throw or corner space to call its own, and you will find that it has a preference for the prettier feeding bowl or the more comfortable car to ride in. Should you wonder why? Not with a **2** animal in your life.

| 2 | 3 | 4 | 5 | 6 | 7 | 8 | 9 | 1 |

A 2 car

If the numbers of your licence plate reduce to **2**, it's a perfect car for you. Just the two of you together – a team with distinctive style and quiet good taste on the road. And, just as the **2** male is quietly handsome without vulgarity or ego, the **2** car – whatever its marque – says 'distinction'.

This vehicle will be a refuge from home, a place to finish novels or read the paper – and, at times, even a place to keep spare shoes and items of clothing. A **2** car is your silent partner – and when you've just got to get up and go, it will be witness to your independence and control over your life. Almost the perfect number, perhaps, for anything on wheels.

1   9   8   7   6   5   4   3   2

YOUR LIFE NUMBER
Your lesson to learn

The time has come to consider the other main number in your numerology chart: your Life Lesson, or LIFE, number. This is sometimes also called the 'Birth Force'. Just as for the DAY number, calculating your LIFE number is easy: simply add together each digit of your full birth date (day, month and year), and keep adding the digits until they reduce to a single number (*see example on page 270*).

And that's it. You have your Life number.
So what does it tell us?

| 2 | 3 | 4 | 5 | 6 | 7 | 8 | 9 | 1 |

What does it mean?

The LIFE number takes times to show its mark. You should see its influence over many years, and understand that it is representative of certain strengths and weaknesses that we learn to live with through years of experience. These characteristics need to be analysed over time, and it can take a while for us to come to know ourselves truly from our LIFE number. Uncovering these aspects of our character is a process of discovery, and we often don't fully recognize the traits of this number as clearly, or as quickly, as those of the stronger DAY number.

Once you have done your sums and discovered this second important number, you'll want to find out what this means. If your LIFE and DAY numbers are the same, this powerfully reinforces the qualities of your own number, and accentuates both strengths and weaknesses. You won't be fighting corners within your personality by having

1   9   8   7   6   5   4   3   2

two numbers to live with that are, perhaps, miles apart in spirit. But then, equally, if your numbers are the same you may lack a broad vision of the world, seeing with very sharp eyes through just a single (though enormous!) window.

On the following pages we will examine what your DAY number 2 is like in tandem with each other number, beginning with the powerful doubling of 2 DAY and 2 LIFE, and then moving on through all other possible combinations. If you discover you have a LIFE number which totals 11 or 22, before it reduces to a final single digit of 2 or 4, read the entry for 2 and 2, or 2 and 4, but also pay special attention to any extra information given relating to the added significance of the number being a variation of a master number.

2 3 4 5 6 7 8 9 1

SAME **DAY** AND **LIFE** NUMBER

With 2 as both of your principal birthday numbers, you are truly one of the most gifted diplomats on the planet! You are probably very gentle much of the time, but the effect of the doubled number — especially if one of them is **11** — is to make you all the more persuasive and convincing. Brave soul, indeed, who would try to pull against you when you have decided to take on a cause or win a battle. No one, perhaps, can win others over more than you. Even though you have such a heightened sensitivity, you are very well directed in where you are going and what you want to achieve, and have an excellent talent for analysis, which helps you break down tasks into realizable portions.

| 1 | 9 | 8 | 7 | 6 | 5 | 4 | 3 | 2 |

If one of the numbers is **11**, your success in life comes from being proud of what you want to do, having dignity and a sense of quality that sets you apart from the crowd. And you have a luminous spiritual essence of being which makes others take notice of you, and turn to you often for guidance. You are sympathetic without being wishy-washy, and your clarity and charm disguises the power you exercise quietly over others. **11**, then, as one of the numbers, would add a serious boost of impetus to the otherwise gentle traits of the **2**, and you will certainly want to achieve an aesthetic refinement in your life, and emanate a sense of graciousness towards both friends and family.

Double trouble?

You do have some blemishes, of course, but they are not ominous. A double **2** (or **2/11**) will be very sensitive to

2 | 3 | 4 | 5 | 6 | 7 | 8 | 9 | 1

criticism, and will hate to feel left out of the plans of someone dear. If you are forgotten for any reason – even without a hint of malice – you will be deeply hurt. If a friend forgets your birthday, or they omit to return a call or an invitation to dinner, you may make much more of it than you should.

Be aware that this is a tendency in your own make-up that you must challenge, and give others the benefit of the doubt – reminding yourself that no one sees into the minds of others quite as well as you can. You must also guard against the extremist part of your nature, and soften the part of you that is too definite in your likes and dislikes.

As **2** is a feminine number, there will be a special radiance in your character which attracts and reassures women. Always bear this in mind, for it should affect you positively in both business and friendships, and help you to know where your best allies are found. Women will, on the whole, be lucky for you; and you will discover you have great, if gentle, leadership qualities with women, who will mostly be very co-operative with you. And if you are a woman, you will have a special allure for men, who are likely to be strongly attracted to your grace and your good taste.

Keep it clean

A double **2** will prove that cleanliness is important to them. Do you have beautiful soaps, and like to pamper yourself with fine toiletries? And this includes the men – who also put a premium on good grooming. Neatness, too, is something you prioritize, and you will be unhappy working in a sloppy or disarrayed space, so whoever lives with, or around, you has to cope with your acute need for things to be perfect, clean and tidy.

The force of both numbers intensifies the irritation

you may feel over little things — like an oyster going over an uncomfortable grain of sand to make the pearl for the sake of improvement. And so it is with you, gradually smoothing the faults or sharp corners in your world and creating something fine because of the drive to do so.

Speak up!

Double **2**, or **2** with **11**, gives you an exaggerated need for peace. When you sense a storm brewing around you emotionally, you will probably retreat into your own world and, to some degree, you never quite emerge. Certain people will always make you feel defensive, and there may be few people you really admire and feel safe with — though you could have many acquaintances and friends.

Trusting someone is important, and you may forgive but never quite forget if someone you love turns on you in a moment of anger. However, if you don't express the hurt you feel, you will live without a soul knowing why you seem to have pulled away from reality and gone into a more spiritual or metaphysical place. This confuses those who love you, and it will be worth talking gently to them. For, after all, your powers of speech and your attitude of conviction are mesmerizing. Use them!

DIFFERENT **DAY** AND **LIFE** NUMBERS

Most of us will find that we have two different birthday numbers, and this can be an advantage. One number may soften the single track of the other, and mean we can see other people's viewpoints more easily. At other times, though, the numbers may be in real conflict – and this leads to vacillation in our reactions to everyday situations, or confusion about why we want to run one way and then another.

In the following pages you will discover how your own two numbers are likely to work together, and what you can do to maximize the potential of both when they are paired up.

1 9 8 7 6 5 4 3 2

2 Day with 1 Life

Overall, this is a fortuitous blend of a stronge and a gentle number. **1** tells us you have good ideas and energies, but you can become dictatorial and dominating sometimes. **2** assuages this, helping you to consult others and intuit their viewpoint. On the other hand, **2** sometimes gets bogged down by too much self-consciousness and attention to negative detail, and **1** can overcome this. **2**'s worst failing – the inclination to dissipate time – is remedied by the boldness of a **1** LIFE number.

Much of your personal sense of style is dictated by your LIFE number, and the power and charisma of the **1** balances the shyness of the gentler and more retiring **2**. **1** helps you emit an outward capability and self-sufficiency, but your **2** DAY number makes it easy for others to approach you and see you as friendly rather than overawing. Your two num-

2	3	4	5	6	7	8	9	1

2 DAY WITH 1 LIFE

bers are complementary, male and female, and help you project a gentle but positive persona. Your LIFE number still ensures that you are highly individualistic in your desires, inclinations and fashion sense and taste, but **2** helps you to adjust to circumstances, and understand how to consult other people about what is required. In short, **2** makes you more flexible and offsets some of that **1** aggression.

Both numbers are creative, and the musicality of **2** suggests you might have real talent in this area, because of the **1**'s singularity of mind and its ability to compose or invent. You will have excellent rhythm, and probably be a good dancer, and you also know how to relate well creatively to another individual being. More importantly, you are much more patient than a **1** is generally, and you will take whatever time is required to learn a skill and utilize it. The patience bestowed on you by the number **2** is one of the blessings of having these numbers together, as is the advantage of understanding how to co-operate with others.

1   9   8   7   6   5   4   3   2

If your **2** is actually an **11**, the **1** intensifies your very good eye for design and line, as **1** also loves original creations. You probably prefer subtle designer clothes and unusual items, and hate to be dressed just like everyone else, but you are ready to put on pastel – or even neutral – colours, with the harmony that comes from these two numbers. Your choice of colour may be daring and, as an **11**, you are more unafraid than any other **2** to draw attention to yourself socially through your choice of style. You marry discretion with flair, and never want to look bland!

The numbers **1** and **11/2** together will sometimes pull you in opposite directions – **1** making you courageous, but **11** very sensitive to nuance, and cautious. If you are mildly eccentric as a result of this disparity, you may choose clothes and interior decoration in your home or office just to shock others, and this sometimes goes deliberately beyond the limits of what a plain **2** would consider tasteful. But you may just carry it off!

| 2 | 3 | 4 | 5 | 6 | 7 | 8 | 9 | 1 |

2 Day with 3 Life

These two numbers are sometimes at loggerheads when they meet as two individuals, but operating within one personality they usually find much better expression. **2** has the kind of good taste and quiet dignity that lends gravity to **3**, which can often be boisterous on its own; and **3** gives **2** a little more pluck, and courage to stand up and say what it wants. Both numbers are popular in different spheres, so the effect of both together is to make a personality with radiance, energy *and* serenity when it matters. Quite a package!

3 pulls **2** through the hedge when it feels like retiring, and adds vigour to the spiritual qualities of the **2**. And if the **2** is actually **11**, this will feel even more the case, for **3** really is like a pep pill that fuels **11**'s physical stamina and helps to make a business or an achievement out of what

1   9   8   7   6   5   4   3   2

may be just an inspired spiritual dream. And then, too, **3** is aided by **2** being more still and, sometimes, quiet in terms of thinking, so that the impact of both numbers together is of a beautiful and harmonious flower garden organized in a symphony of whites and creams of perfect height and shape — now and then made dramatic with a splash of colour. The mental energies, people skills, speaking ability, creative flair — all gain an infusion of colour from the existence of **3** with the number **2**.

The one potential glitch with a **2** DAY and a **3** LIFE number coming together is that **2**'s wonderful organizational ideas can get a bit lost behind too much talk or too many possibilities. **3** is a chatterer and an entertainer, given to some degree of exaggeration, while **2** needs calm to tackle so many tasks in both the private and the career domain. Having such a strong **3** can make **2** lose its certainty and direction. On the whole, though, the numbers complement each other, and make **2** more resilient and less affected by the moods or imagined slights of others. Thus, in life generally, the two numbers emit positivity and charm to such a degree that you are likely to be spoiled for choice with friends, business associates and — yes — lovers too! ... And so the indecision that is latent in **2** but prevalent in **3** really comes to the fore. But how funny you are to listen to, talking about it!

The talents of both numbers are predominantly creative, so a likely career direction is in the area of the arts or working with people in publicity or public relations. Fashion will be interesting for you too, and the **3** draws out **2**'s ability to entertain in many spheres. But don't be surprised if deciding where to place all your energies is not so straightforward, and choice — once again — becomes almost a bane!

2 Day with 4 Life

Anyone with this combination of numbers is going to be hard-working and very well-organized mentally. You really know how to put method into any suggested direction, and **2** adds a sparkle to the otherwise dry **4** (which, on its own, can often annoy others just a little). **2** relieves **4** on a daily basis from being too grinding and serious, for **2** is often playful and **4** needs something to help it laugh and unwind. The two numbers together, then, lend each other something good.

With a **4 LIFE** number, you are going to get through many things in your life, because **4** dislikes leaving anything in the realms of dreams. **4**'s challenge is to make things possible, and this, married to a **2 DAY** number, gives the slightly dreamy side to your character a reality check. **4** never lets a really good opportunity get away from lack

2   3   4   5   6   7   8   9   1

of drive to see it through. Your strong inclination, from your **2 DAY** number, is to place your energies with your home and family, and give as much support as you can to those you love. **4** helps here, as it brings common sense into play. **4** knows when to leave a partner or family member alone to make their own decisions, where **2** occasionally pushes the loved one into a corner and offers to do too much. This is well-meaning, of course, but **4** is stoic and knows when to pull back, creating a sense of balance between the caring qualities and interfering instincts that can make **2**s suffocate those they love. And **2** stops **4** from ignoring what is going on in a loved one's heart. This is a good compromise.

With the maturity that comes with age, and fortifies the qualities of the **4**, material security is likely to come to you. Both numbers like to be able to afford material things, but it is **4** that brings an excellent, practical head to the planning table, and makes it clear how to achieve what you want without selling your soul. These two numbers suggest your home and garden will be an investment but also a respite from the encroaching world.

If the **4** is a **22**, you are on your way to serious achievement that will affect many more people than just yourself. You create a standard of high endeavour, and there is a knock-on effect whereby others you come into contact with feel changed or inspired to new horizons as a direct result of your example. And **22** is a very clever number, which benefits from having the **2** as a daily influence, allowing your intuition to step in at the highest level and add a sharpness to your mind.

Politics seems such a likely place for you to exercise your skills, because **2** is the diplomat and **4** (especially **22**s) the number which works for the social good. It's a lot to live up to, but this combination will do something rather unique in life.

2 Day with 5 Life

Two birthday numbers which are a little at odds, the marriage of **2** and **5** in your personality will make you unpredictable to many – even yourself! **5** asks you to live life to the full, to make a splash and go after what you want, whereas **2** can be shy and more personally retiring. **2**'s good sense and lack of self is quite different to **5**'s sexy personal style – its instinct to say and do what it wants, and laugh at those who don't approve. **2** would rather be a lot less trouble, and retire into the background. So which number will dominate?

The **DAY** number will always be the first to express itself, but, in the case of these two numbers, it's likely that you will feel introverted one minute and quite outgoing the next – so life around you will never be dull, or run to a guaranteed course! **5** adds energy and momentum to **2**,

1 9 8 7 6 5 4 3 2

pushing you to speak up when you feel something strongly – which you so often do. And **5**'s ability to put things into words and finish every sentence with a quip can be good for **2**, as the **2** gives you such insight into people and situations. The effect of both numbers can therefore be entertaining as well as frighteningly on the ball.

5 lends you physical strength and a healthy dose of hardiness. Also, the effect of **5** with **2** intensifies your powers of sexual attraction and, quite probably, your physical appetite in relationships. Across the pattern of your life, as you get older, the **5** LIFE number will have an invigorating impact, for **2** is prone to nervousness and headaches – even to illness caused from emotional upsets. **5** does much to lessen the effect of emotions on your health – although you will undoubtedly live off quite an amount of nervous energy as a legacy from both numbers. Be careful about wearing yourself thin at times, when you feel particularly charged sensually or very much in love; you will give your all and suffer the consequences later, for **5** is daring and **2** can have the propensity for extremes. Mostly, though, through many little spills and thrills, the **2** calms the chaos of **5**, while the **5** makes suppliant **2** a little more demanding.

You may have a distinctive style, with a modulated appreciation for what is traditional whipped up by a preference for more modern design. Your **LIFE** number likes what is new, and **2** can be very happy with clean lines and muted colours, so your taste will have an interesting edge and always amaze the people around you. Sometimes what excites you will surprise you – but the lightning bolt of feeling you get from **5** will make you more adventurous. **5** shakes you up a bit, and helps you take chances in every way. This is especially good for you intellectually, and you could be very progressive and inspiring to your family, and to those who listen to you at work.

2 Day with 6 Life

These numbers are made for each other, and will entice the best qualities in each to greater performance, working in tandem for you. **6** is so creative and peace-loving, and has, like **2**, such good taste and an artistic eye, that it is hard to imagine you would be drawn to do anything else but work in an artistic career. Music, acting, painting are talents that come with each number, so when these numbers come together they will have a very strong impact, and highlight such talents artistically in so many different areas. Both **6** and **2** are numbers that make good teachers, health workers, community professionals, and these fields of opportunity may also attract you vocationally.

What a loving home you will create, and what a concentration on the *needs* of those you love. Surely, with this pair of numbers, you will spoil your children, support their

2   3   4   5   6   7   8   9   1

dreams, stand up for them when they suffer injustice? And challenging your mind will also seem crucial, because both **6** and **2** like to get their teeth into research and reading – perhaps only marginally less than **2** with **7**. **2** and **6** together make a person who is both dreamy and a dream-maker; you are attentive to what is in the minds, hopes and hearts of the people around you, and you'll spend time and energy constantly trying to make wishes really come true for someone you love … for which reason, you may sometimes be a little extravagant financially, or never know when enough is actually enough!

These two numbers are generally so agreeable that it is hard to imagine how they could have anything but a serene and beautiful impact on a person's character, as they come together to influence you. Most at fault, then, might be that **6** and **2** are a little too passive, or that these numbers fail to prop each other up with any aggression – which can be needed sometimes. Or, it may be that you are too idealistic and gullible, at times. But this seems a small price to pay for the gifts of charm, taste, creativity and understanding that come with your numbers, so try to surround yourself with those who won't take too much advantage, but will simply be honoured to share your calm and gracious space, and just to live near you.

Being a number combination that will prioritize entertaining and having company, or being a really good cook rather than just a competent one, make sure you don't overdo your lifestyle with too much good food or soft living. It is, perhaps, the worst danger that comes from both numbers together — especially if the **2** is an **11**.

2 Day with 7 Life

You may not, according to some of your friends, be altogether realistic about life, for the **7** will make you reach even higher than the **2** to the world of perfection and personal thought. 'Retreat', actually, in all of its meanings, is a good keyword for this pair of numbers. **7**s retreat from a world if things are less than they should be – if people don't strive enough for excellence and truth, or if situations are less vivid in reality than in the planning. **2** shares this idealism, and often shrinks, more than retreats, from those who let them down. But this is to emphasize only the troubled waters between these numbers, because the strengths that come with the **2** in your birthday are exceptional.

You will be high-minded and have an inherent nobility about you. Friends, loves and co-workers see you as apart

1   9   8   7   6   5   4   3   2

from the dross, and understand that you are sensitive to injustices. You are a champion of the weak and the poor, and feel that the human race owes it to the planet always to behave like a gracious guest – though you are more than aware that this is rarely the case, and so you often feel let down by the true picture. But, with luck, you never quite give up hope that something can be done to make things better. Refined, deep-thinking, spiritual and philosophical, your two numbers ask that you lead a life of service to others, and that responsibilities sit with you over many years. And you give all of this without too much complaint.

The number **7** sharpens the perceptions of the number **2**, so that you become a specialist. **7** combats **2**'s indecisiveness, and you will go out on a limb to learn everything you can about a subject. You move from teacher to professor, doctor to consultant, musician to soloist, and need to discover the best skills you have and be at the

| 2 | 3 | 4 | 5 | 6 | 7 | 8 | 9 | 1 |

top of your game. Writing may be a considerable talent for you too.

2 loves its family, but 7 often enforces the need of some solitude, so you may have a smaller family or find a way to live both with and away from those you love. This time is needed for your mind to dwell on what is important. Neither 2 nor 7 is a selfish number, so you will possibly feel tugged to perform many acts of kindness or charity for others, or simply to work in a selfless field. Research is likely to be at least a part of what you do. And, with these two numbers working with you, your life will be lived at a high level of professionalism in everything you do. Make sure you have trees, or a view of the sea, to counter the stress you put yourself under.

1   9   8   7   6   5   4   3   2

2 Day with 8 Life

2 and **7** may be the numbers of talent, thinking and perfection, but they lack the killer instinct to get on with some things that need doing. This, you have! **8** coupled with **2** gives you a crucial awareness of living in the material world and, while you are genuinely generous and make life as comfortable for those near you as you can, you do have a sense of self – far more so than **2** and **7** – that pushes you to get on in this world and be a voice to be heard. This very often means that you will make your mark more than the foregoing pair of numbers, even though they also have so much to offer together. **8** lends you forcefulness and drive, and even creates some tension with the **2** because it recognizes that being selfless and undemanding can be difficult for everyone. The **8** helps you ask for what you want and makes you a highly effec-

2   3   4   5   6   7   8   9   1

tive spokesperson in all courts. Your excellent instincts are now backed up by great judgement and the will to make things happen.

These numbers bestow serious musical ability and an appreciation for the rhythms of life, so that the talents of **2** may be honed efficiently through the **8 LIFE** number. Equally, you may have an excellent sense of smell or a refined palate. **2** and **8** together generally improve one of the senses besides hearing, so you may be working very strongly through your physical awarenesses.

Hard work will not frighten you off, and, more than with any other **2** pairing, having an **8 LIFE** number is likely to push you to work for yourself — especially with a partner, or in a string of diverse partnerships. Many will give up trying to keep up with you, but you know where you want to go, and you want to have fun getting there. You may — with that sense of rhythm — also be very good at sport, and physical release in sport, or through outdoor activity, is necessary to balance the energies you use to push yourself mentally.

Relationships are important to you, and you want to be in love with someone who is a little bit special, out of the ordinary. This may not be someone whom everyone agrees is beautiful, but it will be someone you know is striking, and other opinions don't matter. Your destiny is to be in the world talking about something you are passionate about, and this you will do successfully. Your partner has to accept that they will be sharing you – and this is all the more true if your **2** is an **11**. Life will be full, that's for sure!

2 Day with 9 Life

Life has awarded you complementary birthday numbers. Both are feelers, both imaginative, both have a warm heart and a spiritual soul. As a **9 LIFE** number dictates the ultimate direction of your **2** talents, you are likely to travel a great deal, write, speak to many different people and possibly learn a few languages. Your path will not be straight, but it will be eventful and interesting, and you will be known to hundreds – if not thousands.

Your talents are sizeable, and you will have many friends who all have a claim on your time and your affections. **9** makes you more romantic, even heroic, and your personal charisma will help you generate interest in matters you think important to spend your time on – quite often, something with a philanthropic tone. **2** cares so deeply for ordinary people, **9** for the whole of humankind,

1   9   8   7   6   5   4   3   2

so you will place a burden on yourself to be sure that your time on earth is well spent. Sometimes, though, your compassionate nature will make extreme demands on you, and with both **2** and **9** colouring your personality you will often become depressed and saddened by others' short-sightedness or bigotry. The **9**, though, helps focused **2** become a broader thinker, and allows you time to recover and bounce back from the dramas that can occur in frequent cycles and cause you pain.

In matters of the heart you give your feelings passionately, and ask that your partner does the same, but you have a forgiving side to your nature that **2** by itself sometimes lacks, as **9** can think outside the sense of personal injury. For this reason you are loyal to the one you care for, and a sense of compassion and understanding makes you bigger-hearted than perhaps your partner will be.

The worst attribute of the number **2** coming together with **9** is that you may suffer from doubt and vacillation more than you should for someone with your clever mind. **2** can be indecisive at times, and **9** moody, so this energy can undermine your willpower. However, you feel and intuit very acutely what is going on around you, and mostly you will be able to remedy time lost with judicious approaches for a second time. Vocationally, you will be very good at drama, good with words, and, again, teaching or related professions are natural for you. More than any other **2**, don't be surprised if the appearance of the **9** means you will live abroad – or at a distance from your birthplace – for at least some of your life. This will be true even more strongly if you are an **11** – and, in this last case, you are likely to find some fame in this world, as well. Or have you already?

1   9   8   7   6   5   4   3   2

THE FUTURE
Take a look what's in store...

And now we come to the calculation of your future. Each year, on your birthday, you move into a new sphere of number-influence which governs that year. The numbers progress in cycles of nine years; after nine years, the cycle starts over again, and a whole new period of your life begins afresh. The cycle can be applied to every number, so you can discover what the main issues will be for partners, friends and family, as well as for yourself, in any given year (*see calculation instructions, opposite*). Emphasis is placed on what will happen to you when you are in your own year number – that is, in any '2' year cycle.

| 2 | 3 | 4 | 5 | 6 | 7 | 8 | 9 | 1 |

Working out your cycle

To find out what year you're currently in, use the same formula employed for calculating the **LIFE** number, but substitute the current year for the year in which you were born. Every year, the cycle then moves on by one more number until, after a **9** year, returning to **1**, to begin the cycle again.

Calculation example 1

BIRTHDAY: 29 April 1961

TO CALCULATE THE CURRENT YEAR NUMBER: $2+9+4+\underbrace{[2+0+0+7]}_{\text{CURRENT YEAR}} = 24$, and $2+4 = $ **6**

*This means that on 29 April 2007 you move into a **6** year. On 29 April the following year, this would then move into a **7** year ($2+9+4+2+0+0+8 = 25$, and $2+5 = $ **7**), and the year after that, an **8** year, and so on.*

1	9	8	7	6	5	4	3	2

Calculation example 2

> BIRTHDAY: 20 September 1980
>
> TO CALCULATE THE
> CURRENT YEAR NUMBER: $2+0+9+\boxed{2+0+0+7}=20$, and $2+0=\mathbf{2}$
> CURRENT YEAR

*This means that on 20 September 2007 you move into a **2** year. On 20 September the following year, this would then move into a **3** year (2+0+9+2+0+0+8 = 21, and 2+1 = **3**), and the year after that, a **4** year, and so on.*

Many numerologists feel that the impact of a year number can be felt from the first day of that year – in other words, from 1st January. However, the usual school of thought is that the new number cycle is initiated *on your birthday itself*, and my experience tends to corroborate this. So, if your birthday is fairly late in the year – November or December, say – this means that you will have gone through most of the calendrical year before *your* new

| 2 | 3 | 4 | 5 | 6 | 7 | 8 | 9 | 1 |

number-year cycle for that year begins.

Look back over some recent years, and see if – in the descriptions on the following pages – you can pinpoint the moment when your yearly number-cycle for any given year became apparent. You'll be amazed at just how accurate this system seems to be.

A 1 year

This is the perfect time to set up new and quite specific long-term goals, and consider just where you want to be a few years from now. You will have new people around you from this point on, and fresh ideas about them and the interests they awaken in you. This is a completely new chapter in your life, and you should set goals for a better and more fulfilling future.

Career-wise, a **1** year often occurs at a time of new employment, or of a complete change in direction in your working life. You are probably wanting to develop new skills or make use of untested talents. You have to believe in yourself now. This is the time when it's a little easier to step back and see how to get started along a particular path. Goals, you will understand, are perfectly attainable, even if a year ago they seemed unrealistic. In a **1** year you have tremendous focus and independence, and excellent determination.

The secret to your success now is in your ability to concentrate; but, emotionally, things can be quite testing. No matter how strong a love bond may be in your life, a **1** year demands that you do much for yourself. You could feel isolated or unsupported, even if someone dear is close by. This is a test of your own courage and inner strength. Only your strongest desires will gain results ... but then, your desires should be fierce during this cycle. Try not to act impulsively, as the push to do so will be powerful, but also, don't be afraid to be independent and go your own way. Strong urges are driving you — forward, for the most part — and a **1** year lends you exceptional clarity and energy.

A 2 year

A year which demands co-operation and partnerships at every level, **2** is a gentle year cycle, when you can consolidate what you started in the previous twelve months. Being a **2**, it suits you very soundly. You will need to be diplomatic and sensitive towards other people's feelings, which is easy for you, and your intuition is very strong now, so that you are able to share the load and the initiative more than you were allowed last year. For this reason, don't try to push things too far or too fast. After the previous whirlwind year, this is a moment to take your time and get things right.

Relationships come more into focus during a **2** year. This is especially pleasing if someone new entered your life in the last year or so, for the vibration of **2** helps a bond to strengthen, and a feeling of mutuality improves

2   3   4   5   6   7   8   9   1

now. In some ways you may feel the desire or the need to be secretive, but this is because there are unknown elements at work all on fronts. It will affect you at work and at play, and in a close tie you will discover new tenderness that will probably separate you from other friends. If there is no one special currently in your life, this may be the year to find someone: a **2** year brings a relationship much stronger than a fling!

Your negotiation skills and ability to guess what another person is feeling may work very well for you this year; and, if the number **2** derives from master number **11** (which it almost surely will), there is a chance for serious partnerships and master opportunities. You will need to look at contracts carefully, and spend time on legalities. But this is often the most exciting and unusual year out of the nine. Mysteries come to light, and your ideas flow well. Just be prepared to consider another person in every equation.

A 3 year

Time for you! This twelve-month period is concerned with developing your abilities and testing your flexibility. Your imagination is especially strong, and you may have particular opportunities to improve your wealth and make lasting friendships. You will also need to be focused, because the energy of a **3** year is fast and furious, and may make you feel dissolute. Usually, though, this is a happy year spent with some travel prospects and many creative inspirations. Difficulties which intruded in the previous two years are often resolved in this year cycle.

Business and your social life often run together in a **3** year, and work will be a lot of fun. It is worth taking time over your appearance and indulging yourself more than usual, for the sociability of this number brings you many invitations and a chance to create a new look, or to explore

2   3   4   5   6   7   8   9   1

other aspects of your personality. You have extra charm this year, so try to use it where it is needed.

Many people find that the number **3** expresses itself in a year cycle as a third person to consider: frequently, this is the birth of a child or an addition to the family, but it might be that another party pressures you in your personal relationship. Don't talk too much about this, or show nervousness. Under a **3** vibration, it is easy to become exhausted – even through over-excitement – so be alert to the impulse towards extravagance and fragmentation. Try to enjoy the way in which you are being drawn out of yourself this year, and allow yourself time to study, write, paint. Anything you really want you can achieve now – even strange wishes and desires can be pulled towards you. Make sure you think a little about what you are asking for!

| 1 | 9 | 8 | 7 | 6 | 5 | 4 | 3 | 2 |

A 4 year

A much-needed year of good-housekeeping – on the personal level, as well as literally. This year will demand practicality from you. Often a **4** brings a focus on money or accounts, on repairs around the home, or on putting your life into better order. It may not be what you want, yet it will force itself upon you. It is sometimes a year spent with a pen in hand – writing lists or cheques, doing sums and keeping diaries. It is also a year when you will need to do some research, to find out about what you don't know.

You have so much work to do in a **4**, or **22**, year – more than for a long time. Your personal pleasure takes second place to requirement, and it may seem difficult to stick to the task sometimes. Money demands that you do so, for extra expenditure is not advised in this twelve-month period. Yet if this sounds stressful, it also gives you a feeling of satisfaction that you will achieve so much this year – a job of hard work and dedication really well done. It may be that this year gives you a very good foundation for the future and sets up lasting improvements.

You will never survive a **4** – or, especially, a **22** – year if you are not organized and implement a system of work and life. Be honest in what you do with others, but also in what you do for yourself. You cannot deceive yourself, and must check details carefully. You may have a feeling of burden at times, but there is a chance to feel you have done something extraordinary too. Translate your clever ideas into practical results. The most significant thing for you to do is to concentrate on proper personal management. The weight of the world is on your shoulders, but you can bear it if the preparations you make are good. There is no escape from demands on your time and intelligence, but nothing can be hurried, so face the job ahead and you will soon find you have climbed a hill to new vistas.

A 5 year

After careful management of your time last year, and a feeling of being tied to the wheel, this will seem like bursting from the inside of a darkened room into bright light. Now you have a change from routine to madness, and you may feel a personal freedom that was denied you last year. Nevertheless, nothing is completely settled in a **5** year, and this uncertainty may take its toll. Try to look at this cycle as a chance to find success in newer areas, and a way to advance from necessary stagnation into running waters of energy and vitality. You will update your sense of yourself during this period, and make progress towards the life you want, following the previous year's required self-discipline.

You are admitting to the need for new pastures, so your ideas of what your life might include, or who may have a role in it, may alter now. No one likes to be held back in

2   3   4   5   6   7   8   9   1

a **5** year, but it is still important not to be too hasty in your actions. Use your energies, by all means, but govern them with your head. This is the time for innovation, and new takes on old goals, but if you quarrel with those dear to you, or with whom you work, it may be difficult to repair later. If change is still inevitable, be as kind and constructive as possible, and make sure you aren't leaping from one difficult situation straight into another. You need to discover your versatility and personal resourcefulness to get the best out of this cycle. And, for some of the twelve months, travel or lots of movement seems inescapable.

This year is potentially some kind of turning point for you. Learning how to adapt to sudden circumstances is vital, because any plans or directives set in stone will cause you pain, and possibly come unstuck. Be prepared for changes and, if this brings a nervousness with it, try to meet the adventure head-on. If you talk yourself up and take on a front-running position, you can work wonders in a **5** year.

1 9 8 7 6 5 4 3 2

A 6 year

Love is in the air. Other things seize your time too – your home needs attention, and duties demand your energy – but, principally, this year is about emotions and relationships. Sometimes love and happiness are a reward for surviving so much in the past two years, and for unselfish service and support for others. The emphasis is on finding harmony with others, and this may come in various ways. This year, you may have the impetus and opportunity to erase problems that have previously beset you. You understand, and feel acutely sensitive towards, others, and are more radiant and beautiful than you have been for some time. If you can be kind and positive in emotional dealings, you will benefit in many ways, including materially.

There are hurdles in a **6** year in connection with obligations you feel towards others. At times you are stretched, because there are personal desires and ties you want to nurture which are countermanded by the duties you are subjected to. You may resent this, yet, if you can remain cheerful, you will be rewarded in ways not immediately apparent. Love is trying to sweep you off your feet, but your health may suffer because you are trying to fit in so much, and the intensity of your feelings is strong.

While it's good to be helpful in a **6** year, don't allow yourself to be taken advantage of, or let people drain you completely. Set up a system that lets you delegate some responsibility. Your home may bloom while you're in such a happy mood, and you should feel creative and mellow. The events of a **6** year are not as fast and furious as the previous year, but things move steadily towards a happier state of being. Let the time go as it will, because this is not a year to fight against what comes to you; get into the right philosophical gear and open yourself to pleasant surprises that come from being useful, and being warm with others.

1   9   8   7   6   5   4   3   2

A 7 year

This year is a time for manifesting your goals by visualizing them. See yourself triumphing and continuing toward your vision. Never lose sight of what you want, or confusion will reign. You'll be tempted this way and that, annoyed by gossip, and attacked by those who love you but don't understand what you are trying to do. Don't be swayed by them, or you will lose your opportunities and precious time.

Keep your head, as everything depends on your state of mind. Refuse to react to distractions, and avoid hasty actions or sudden decisions. A calm approach is the best remedy to the chaos surrounding you. You may have to move house without warning, but take it in your stride and make a calm, clear choice on where to go. If you are travelling somewhere exotic, be prepared with vitamins and medicines to avoid viruses of any kind.

Legal matters may arise during this year, relating to business, investments or house options. Consult an expert to avoid pitfalls, and, when you feel happy, proceed with confidence. If you have taken all the facts and details into account, you'll now be within sight of your goal. But watch your health, as the number **7** is connected with this subject for both good and ill. You might get fit and lose some weight or, conversely, suffer with some little grievance. This is a time for mental, spiritual and physical detoxing. Also, rest: take a vacation to the country, to a quiet location where you can think in peace. Let no one confuse you. You may have to wait, but you will know how to come out on top if you listen to your intuition.

This is an excellent year for study, research, writing and reading, and clearing out all the unnecessary people or ideas from your past.

1   9   8   7   6   5   4   3   2

An 8 year

This cycle brings the possible finding of a soulmate. If you're single, you could not have a better chance of meeting that special someone than now. **8** years also relate to money, so you may be caught up with an impossible workload and regard the arrival of such a potentially strong love as poor timing – and perhaps this is why it comes to you, because your attention being taken up elsewhere may be the best reason for someone's admiration. The love vibration you experience under karmic year number **8** may point to a future relationship prospect which has a lasting importance.

For those in settled relationships, pregnancy sometimes comes with this number, and it brings a very special link between the child and their parents. Or, you may experience a deep urge to study a subject that comes easily to you, though you have never learned about it before – a

2 3 4 5 6 7 8 9 1

language, perhaps, or an artistic skill you were attracted to but never developed, but which you now pick up well. Even a professional subject that you seem to grasp quickly will seem more important to perfect than ever before. Partly, this is because **8** year cycles concern making more money, and dealing with the deeply felt past. There are huge opportunities for you in an **8** year, and you will want to be prepared to maximize them. However, you'll need to use good judgement and be efficient with your time management.

Many people feel pushed to the limit in an **8** year, because there is just so much going on. Consider, though, that the vibration of the number wants to find positive expression, so the more efficiency and determination you can bring to it, the better the chance of finishing on a high note. Don't over-commit your time or money, and be ready to acquiesce to others' ways of doing things. You need to be confident, but ready to adjust too. **8** is made up of two circles, asking 'infinity' of you. But this year, you can do it!

1   9   8   7   6   5   4   3   2

A 9 year

Your personal affairs all come to a head in a **9** year, and whatever has been insufficient, or unsatisfying, will rise to the surface and demand change now. It could be the fulfilment of many dreams, for this is the culmination of nine years' experience. Whatever is jettisoned was probably no longer of use – though this might seem dispassionate. Many friendships will drift away, but you have probably outgrown them. The strongest demand of you is a readiness to discard what will not be part of your serious future – and this can mean a temporary feeling of insecurity.

You will certainly travel in a **9** year. Even if a trip is short, or of no great distance, it will settle something in your mind. The more compassionate, tolerant and forgiving you are, the more warmth and generosity will come to you. This is not the right moment to start something com-

2   3   4   5   6   7   8   9   1

pletely new, but if events arise as a natural conclusion to what has gone before, this is a good thing. Your mind needs to engage with bigger issues, for selfishness or petty ideas will cause you unhappiness under this number. People will thwart you in your career and personal matters – and these obstacles seem to come out of the blue, and are beyond your control. However, if you think on philosophical issues and remain open to big ideas, everything will turn out well.

A **9** year can be populated with many friends and activities, yet can feel lonely too; this is a cycle for completion of tasks and the ending of what is not enduring. But this is the right time to see the fruits of your previous work. Be wise about where your destiny seems to want to take you. Your artistic and imaginative facilities are inspired now, and you'll begin to see new directions that you know you must investigate in the years ahead. You know what is missing in your life, or where you've failed yourself, and can now prepare for the new adventure that's about to dawn.

1   9   8   7   6   5   4   3   2

How to find your DAY NUMBER

Add the digits for the day of birth, and keep adding them until they reduce to one number:

EXAMPLES

29 April 1961   2+9 = 11 (a 'master' number), and 1+1 = **2**

20 September 1980   2+0 = **2**

How to find your LIFE NUMBER

Add the digits for the day, month and year of birth, and keep adding them until they reduce to one number:

EXAMPLES

29 April 1961   2+9+4+1+9+6+1 = 32,
                       and 3+2 = **5**

20 September 1980   2+0+9+1+9+8+0 = 29
                       2+9 = 11 (a 'master' number), and 1+1 = **2**

Further reading

The Complete Book of Numerology, David A. Phillips, Hay House, 2006

The Day You Were Born: A Journey to Wholeness Through Astrology and Numerology, Linda Joyce, Citadel Press, 2003

Many Things on Numerology, Juno Jordan, De Vorss Books, 1981

Numerology, Hans Decoz and Tom Monte, Perigee Books, 2001

Numerology: The Romance in Your Name, Juno Jordan, De Vorss Books, 1977

Sacred Number, Miranda Lundy, Wooden Books, 2006

The Secret Science of Numerology: The Hidden Meaning of Numbers and Letters, Shirley Blackwell Lawrence, New Page Books, 2001

About the author

Titania Hardie is Britain's favourite 'Good Witch' and a best-selling author. Born in Sydney, Australia, Titania has a degree in English and Psychology, and also trained in parapsychology and horary astrology. With a high media profile, she regularly appears on television in the UK, US, Canada, Australia and South Africa, as well as receiving widespread newspaper and magazine coverage. Her previous titles have sold over a million copies worldwide, and include *Titania's Crystal Ball*, *Aroma Magic*, and *Hocus Pocus*. Her first novel is due to be published in summer 2007.

Acknowledgements

Many thanks to you, Nick, for the clear and brilliant vision; you knew what you wanted and, like a true and inspired **1**, kept mulling it over until a way was found. This is your baby. Also big thanks to Tessa, master number **22**, for your commitment to this magnum opus beyond call: only you and I know, Tessa, how much time and soul has gone into all of these words. To Ian, for keeping us piping along with a true **4**'s sanguine approach to such a long body of work, and to Elaine and Malcolm for the look – **6**s, naturally! For my daughter Samantha, thanks for some of your ideas which found expression in the second-to-last section: I love the latte in Soho while signing the author. Let's see! To Georgia, for work in the field on number **5**, my thanks. To all of you, my appreciation, and I wish you all LUCKY NUMBERS!

EDDISON·SADD EDITIONS

Editorial Director **Ian Jackson**
Managing Editor **Tessa Monina**
Proofreader **Nikky Twyman**

Art Director **Elaine Partington**
Mac Designer **Brazzle Atkins**
Production **Sarah Rooney**